Jesse James Wroblewski

—

MARKETING

FOR

SUPER

VILLAINS

Diabolical Tips on Differentiation,
Decommoditization™, and World Domination

ISBN: Paperback 979-8-9890673-0-5
ISBN: Ebook 979-8-9890673-1-2

Design and publishing assistance by The Happy Self-Publisher.

MarketingForSupervillains.com

DEDICATION

For Mola Ram

When it comes to supervillains, Steven Spielberg called Mola Ram "the best the world has ever produced and ever will." Portrayed by Amrish Puri, Mola Ram is the cultist high priest in *Indiana Jones and the Temple of Doom*.

Like all great villains, Mola Ram bent the world to his will. He changed an entire industry as he single-handedly (pun intended) created the need for a new, PG-13 rating from the Motion Picture Association of America.

How? Mola Ram tore a man's heart from his chest in a ceremony while chanting *Kali Ma, shakti de!* ("Mother Kali, give me thy power!")

Mola Ram is my own personal boogeyman. Clients regularly seek me out for my expertise and creativity. Attracted to my nonconformist way of thinking, they plead, "Jesse, take us to the edge!"—only to rip my heart out and turn my designs into boring white noise.

The threat of Mola lurking inside every boardroom, just waiting to rip the life from my creations, is a constant reminder to sharpen my sword and be prepared for battle to defend my work.

Enough. I will no longer conform against my will. After reading this book, neither will you.

To quote the boogeyman himself:

You don't believe me? You will, Dr. Jones. You will become a true believer.

TABLE OF CONTENTS

INTRODUCTION

"We're not so different, you and I."

**—Every supervillain, when they have
their nemesis right where they want them**

Y「ou've probably heard some version of this speech before. Stick with me.

With my superpowers, I can see that you are either a marketing professional or a business owner, moments away from being sacrificed by the infernal death machine called commoditization.

Or maybe you just like horror stories.

All of the stories you are about to hear will hit harder if you play your role to the fullest. You will heed what I say with the utmost gravity when you imagine a powerful laser, inching slowly toward your head. Or a giant circular saw, *this close* to slicing through your tuxedo pants.

Maybe you don't have to pretend at all.

Maybe you already know, all too well, the stress of lying awake as you try to figure out next week's payroll. Or you're scrambling to spin those horrible marketing analytics before your next progress meeting, in a desperate bid to keep your precious client.

So here we are: predator and prey, villain and hero.

While much of this book is intended to provide you with the necessary skills to escape our infernal death machine, some things are just indisputable. When a supervillain (yours truly) has the undivided attention of his ~~victim~~ prey (you), he simply *must* tell every detail of his grand plans.

Supervillains love a good monologue. We're storytellers. It's just what we do.

I was once you, you know.

I've been in marketing for over 20 years: running agencies, consulting with principals, kowtowing to the absurd demands of clients, and tirelessly refining my skills through continued education. Yet I find myself yielding to the whims of my self-obsessed, half-witted influencer clients who have drummed up millions of mindless followers, which, in this insane world, equates to them taking home triple my income.

Am I resentful? You better believe it!

But don't misunderstand me—I've had my fair share of setbacks. Key staff members leaving at inopportune times (is there ever an opportune one?). Sweating two days before payroll because once again, I have to go into my own personal savings to make sure I met my financial obligations to my team. Racking up personal debts under the guise of "reinvestment" because my business had to pay back dividends *someday* . . . didn't it? Subsisting on ramen noodles or skipping meals altogether because I was sick with worry. It was all starting to wear thin.

I've officially had enough, and now my plan is finally coming to fruition.

Admit it—there have been days when you've been in my shoes. Whether you're a seasoned marketing executive or a green newbie charged with marketing your new startup, you've probably had all of these same, cynical thoughts but never verbalized them. Or maybe they may have exited your mouth on occasion or two!

As I use my superpowers to delve into your deepest thoughts, I see that sometime in the not-so-distant past, you've uttered in complete frustration:

"This fucking industry of mine…!"

You see, you and I are not so different. You, my new marketing supervillainous friend, are at a crossroads. It's time to make a choice: lie down and let the industry destroy everything you have put your blood, sweat and tears into building . . . or become a Marketing Supervillain (MSV for short).

You don't know me . . . yet. However, I am willing to bet if you've made it even this far into my diatribe, we'll be kindred spirits.

You see, I was never interested in being commoditized; I have designed and lived my life accordingly. I never looked at life through the same lens as the rest of my fellow humans. I wanted to know how, like the phoenix, I could rise from the ashes, dust myself off, and reignite my personal mission to take over and revolutionize this crazy industry.

I searched for wisdom wherever I could: the carny world, professional wrestling, infomercials, B movies, the world of magicians and mind readers, "weird" musical groups, action figures, and James Bond movies. I looked everywhere . . . *except* the agency world. I deliberately wanted to be the anti-agency, so why would I ever look there for advice? As a matter of fact, the only thing I got from the agency world was to find out exactly how I *didn't* want to proceed, and knowing what you *don't* want can be as much of a guiding GPS as knowing what you do want.

The time has come for us to make order out of this chaotic world of marketing. And now that I have you right where I want you, let's get down to business.

The MSV Masterplan

In this book, you'll learn the skills how to be an effective Marketing Supervillain. The book is broken up into three main parts:

> PART I: WHY anyone would want to become an MSV.
>
> PART II: HOW someone could become an MSV.
>
> PART III: The MOMENT OF TRUTH where I remove all your fears and anxieties that will inevitably come with such a transformation and the associated, monumental task of taking over the world.

Supervillains hate rules, so I'm not going to demand you read this tome in sequential order. But I will recommend it for the most aspiring MSVs, because you'll never know when I may lurk around the corner, ready to pounce and test your knowledge.

You see, you and I are not so different.

You are correct that this effin' industry of yours is doomed, crazy, illogical and, above all, unappreciative of your excellence.

They'll all be sorry. The time has come for you to embrace who you really are and ignite a new era.

The era of *your* success.

The era of *your* brand.

The era of *your* marketing supervillainy.

PART I

THE WHY:

1: LET'S DO THIS

"Let's Do It."

—Gary Gilmore

R evolution is the answer.

To what question? you may ask.

To the question "What do supervillains want?" (Besides a towering solid-gold statue of themselves, of course.) We want revolution!

For far too long, marketers have gotten the short end of the stick. We cater to the crazy, uneducated whims of clients' changes. Worse, we cater to the demands of their left-brained financial analysts or legal teams who, at best, water down our most creative ideas and, at worst, create their own and simply ask us to be order takers for their brain-numbing, white-noise minutiae. Sadly, for many of us to earn a living, this has become a normal and accepted casualty of doing business. And we pay a large price in our creative energy and self-esteem for doing so.

This effin' industry of mine needs a kick in the ass. Need I remind you that marketing is everything? Hell, without marketing, the current powers that be would likely not be in power at all.

Take one of the most egregious examples: Hollywood. Hollywood executives (the moneymen) throw hundreds of millions of dollars into the production budget of a blockbuster movie. They then feel that the prowess of their finances also gives them the liberty to tinker with the very product they hired a team of *creative professionals* to produce. After everyone in the C-suite gets their dirty little fingerprints onto the final product, they realize their movie has become shit.

This effin' industry.

So what do they do? They call in the person who, like *Pulp Fiction*'s Jimmie Dimmick (played by Quentin Tarantino), can make the problem go away. Similar to Harvey Keitel's cold-blooded, hardened character Mr. Wolf, who can clean up any mess, it is our marketing brethren who are summoned.

We create the movie posters and the trailers. We manufacture the buzz to help the bigwigs recoup their investments and hopefully eke out a profit. Without marketing, Hollywood would simply implode.

Why is it you can easily name Tom Cruise and his latest costar and recite the tagline for the latest summer blockbuster, but you have no idea who meticulously crafted the kickass trailer that got you off your ass and into the theater? Why is there no Academy Award for the marketing forces who are the saviors of an entire industry?

Why do I want an industry revolution?

Because we need to unite, organize, and mobilize. We need to stop rolling over for clients and fight for our creative ideas. At its core, marketing has deep roots in nonconformist thinking and I am taking a stand for more nonconformist ideas to be birthed into the world completely unscathed by client influence.

The debate of superhero or supervillain is simply a matter of perspective. You can say rebels are leaders of a revolution or insurrectionists attempting a coup. You can call them freedom fighters or terrorists.

Batman breaks laws and enforces vigilante justice to safeguard a town gone mad. Some could certainly say he's a villain. Others could see him as heroic—someone who risks their own health and well-being for the benefit of others.

I repeat: *Superhero or supervillain is all just a matter of perspective.*

Unfortunately, the perspective we seem to rely on most is that of the general public. Focus group after focus group, as well as countless scientific studies, have proven beyond a shadow of a doubt that the people have *no idea* what they truly want.

Marketing supervillainy will unquestionably draw fire from the average person. But who cares? You've tried being average, and it sucked.

At the closing of Christopher Nolan's *The Dark Knight*, Lt. James Gordon explains the hero/villain conundrum to a child: "[He's] the hero Gotham deserves, but not the one it needs right now. So we'll hunt him. Because he can take it." Don't be afraid if you are hunted. Instead, exalt in the fact that you so challenge the way things operate that someone feels the need to silence you.

Dan Wieden of the Wieden+Kennedy agency found inspiration in the 1976 story of Gary Gilmore. Nike's slogan "JUST DO IT" had its origin in Gilmore's last words before firing squad execution: "Let's Do It." To be clear, I'm not romanticizing his horrific actions. But for the iconic sneaker company, the call of defiance, in the face of adversity, was exactly what they wanted the spirit of their brand to represent.

According to industry research, more than 95% percent of you holding this book will never make it to the final page. To the remaining, defiant 5% percent who are ready to act, I implore you to pump your fist in the air and join me in the war chant of our revolution, "LET'S DO IT."

Even if its inspiration came from a convicted murderer.

2: THIS EFFIN' INDUSTRY OF MINE

"They think I'm hiding in the shadows . . .
but I AM the shadows."
—The Batman (2022)

I thrive in the shadows.

However, today I seek them for a much different reason. It is the hottest year on record and I find myself in an uncommon, uncomfortable situation: I'm out in public. It's August, I'm in Brooklyn at the Continental Army Plaza, and I am in desperate search of some relief. I find some solace from the oppressive heat in the shadows cast by a towering statue.

The statue is of a man I'm certain you'd never categorize as a supervillain. Ironically, he too preferred the shadows, much like the one he is providing for me now. Even though he was once considered an outsider, I'm willing to bet you've crossed a bridge bearing his name. You've probably visited or lived in a land named after him. At the very least, you definitely have a copy of his visage within reach.

He had pleurisy, as well as dentures created from the teeth of both animals and enslaved people. They caused not only visible physical differences but also affected his speech. He was so convinced others focused solely on his appearance that he rarely spoke and frequently attempted to blend into the background. Feeling shunned by society, he nevertheless remained singularly committed to his mission. Even though he was neither bold nor brash, he was still successful in gathering and convincing legions to go along with his bidding—an impossible feat without the mind of an MSV.

This outcast and his followers launched and led a secret attack against the opposition. It was an almost impossible, unthinkable assault with a treacherous, frozen river between them and victory. It occurred on Christmas Day, 1776.

Sometime after that, this introverted, shadow-dwelling, "wooden-toothed" outsider known as George Washington gained a new moniker: Mr. President.

Like GW, I too have an uncompromising will to win, at any cost. How about you?

Never one to dream of being a cog in a bigger machine or having a boss, I started my own agency in an underground lair on Long Island (aka my mom's basement) and I aimed to build the biggest and best marketing agency on the planet.

The timing was perfect. The internet was becoming ubiquitous. I couldn't gobble up enough knowledge about HTML and the web's inner workings. I'd spend every free moment tearing apart websites to learn what made them tick, what made them successful—or more importantly, what made them fail.

Things progressed and, like a fool, I fell into a common trap: *Do what everyone else was doing, but do it better.* I built a team who knew I accepted nothing short of excellence within my walls. And those walls? They quickly grew, out of mother's dark basement and into the world, purposefully, for all to see.

Big, bright, Apple-esque agency headquarters with pristine white walls, pinball machines, Ping-Pong tables—you know, everything you'd come to expect from a cutting-edge design agency.

My ambition and hunger led me to a bigger arena. Along with that came more "wonderful" clients . . . and more insanity.

The clients would feed my ego and seek out my expertise. I felt proud and useful . . . until they ignored my expert knowledge and, in many cases, did the opposite of what I had strategized for them. I would allow these clients to occupy prime real estate in my brain (rent-free, I might add!). I'd review their cases over and over, on the drive to the office, in the shower, or lying in bed. At times, my wife would catch me distracted and inattentive during our time together as I obsessed over providing the absolute best, most creative solutions to *my* clients' needs.

There were days when I could only surmise that some of these clients were indeed henchmen of a rival competitor, secretly placed inside my business with the singular goal of taking my entire company down, through their insane, illogical requests for changes.

Some patients walk into a doctor's exam room, armed with a self-diagnosis and their own recommendation for a prescription, rather than listening to a professional. (Yeah, I'll just toss you the script pad while I'm at it, since you *clearly* know how to fix all your problems.) My clients were like these nightmare patients. In our meetings, they would *tell* me what they needed, *demanding* social media marketing, SEO, or some other ineffective medicine that ultimately failed (even though they wouldn't listen when I correctly predicted it). Of course, the fault was never their own; it was always on the part of the agency. So they would leave and find a different "yes man" agency that would execute their cockamamie self-prescribed, under-researched, FOMO solution.

And then there were my personal favorites, the clients who were clearly sent here from another dimension to try and torture me. You know, the dimension where time has no meaning or value. A nemesis from this dimension would "request":

"You know that 30-second TV ad we've been finely tuning for the past month? Could you please add these 15 seconds of content without extending the runtime? Oh yeah, and I need it done before lunch."

Even though it clearly defied the laws of time and space, somehow, I always found a way to get it done, but at what cost? My team? My sanity? My relationship with my wife? My own self-worth? My company's profits?

But with a growing crew of committed minions at my side, all of who liked to eat, we grudgingly agreed to the insanity just so we could get that money into the corporate bank account.

In my quest for world domination, I had created a monster that demanded to be fed no matter what had to be done.

My original dream was to build something that would serve me and provide me with a life of luxury and comfort. Instead, I was serving with no benefit at all to myself.

This "world domination" thing was beginning to feel like a job, and a bad-paying one at that. This all seemed like a no-win scenario.

I was living inside my own Kobayashi Maru.

3: THE KOBAYASHI MARU

"I don't believe in no-win scenarios."
—Captain James T. Kirk

The Kobayashi Maru.

Fans will recognize the name from the 1982 film *Star Trek II: The Wrath of Khan*. The Kobayashi Maru is a test that would have guaranteed the destruction of one of two opposing ships and forced cadets to deal with a no-win scenario.

James T. Kirk was the only cadet to ever defeat the Kobayashi Maru. How? Read on and prosper.

Let's face it; business is rigged. Much like the Kobayashi Maru, as you try to build your brand, you'll be faced with seemingly countless no-win scenarios.

- Business is down; it's time to market. But business is down; where do you find a budget for marketing?
- Don't sweat the small stuff, but that small typo in your PowerPoint lost you the deal.

- The early bird gets the worm, but the first mouse gets the guillotine and the second mouse gets the cheese.
- You don't have the staff to support growth, but if you did grow, you could afford the staff. Which comes first?

Whether you are a business owner or a marketer being hired by a brand, you've no doubt encountered a very common no-win scenario where the marketing director says they want to do something completely different, stand out in the crowd . . . you know, "really take it to the edge!"

The edge is where you thrive. But as you gleefully take the client there, they peer over the side, their pulse quickens in panic, and they briskly retreat back to the world of familiar safety. The result: boring, middle-of-the-road marketing that ultimately says nothing anyone remembers.

I've worked with brands of all sizes and sectors, from the local neighborhood realtor to Fortune 50 companies. Not once have I sat in a discovery meeting where the main objective was to "fit in." No one has ever asked me to create mundane, humdrum messaging that gets lost in the white noise of the marketplace. No one *says* they want any of these things . . . but their behavior says different. Loudly.

The human need for belonging, safety and security fits into a tidy cognitive bias called *loss aversion*. Simply put, loss aversion means the psychological pain of losing something feels twice as powerful as the pleasure of gaining something. The overall effect is that it unconditionally destroys creativity.

Brands in need of new marketing or positioning know they need a change but, as we'll discuss further, they also are diametrically opposed to feeling uncomfortable. Change is both hard and uncomfortable. The dire *need* for change switches to a *want* for change, which quickly switches to the *option* of change versus staying safe and maintaining the status quo, which likely got them to where they are currently. The internal dialogue that descends into complacency sounds like this:

"We *have to* do something radical!"

"It would be great *if* we do something."

"What if we do something and it doesn't work?"

"Let's just change a little bit, maybe the colors in our advertising."

If you still think you are the lone unicorn who is immune to these scenarios, consider this: When Apple wanted to push the boundaries by poking the industry beast that was Microsoft with a politically charged angle and release the genius "1984"-themed Super Bowl commercial. It was widely renowned as the best commercial ever made, but the board decided to pull the plug last minute. It was Steve Jobs who had to use his own money to run the ad himself, one time and one time only.

If the marketers at Apple (the most valued company in the world at the time of this writing) who created the greatest commercial ever were not free from this madness, what hope is there for you or me?

A life of honing your skills and being called upon for your expertise only to have it disregarded time and time again can appear like the Kobayashi Maru, a no-win scenario that is certainly enough to drive you right over the edge.

Marketing clients think they want your new and exciting ideas, but what they really want is to have the option on the table while they keep doing what they've always done. The safety of knowing they've *explored* the possibility of change lets them sleep better at night.

Which brings us back to the Kobayashi Maru. How did Kirk defeat it? He reprogrammed the simulation to lean in his favor and ultimately make himself the hero (or the villain, depending on your perspective).

Is the act of changing the rules cheating? Maybe, but if the rules don't say you can't rewrite the rules, then it's not breaking the rules.

Was it effective? Absolutely.

Ultimately Kirk received a commendation from the academy for Creative Thinking. Isn't that what we've all been hanging our entire marketing careers on? We are professional creative thinkers, and the time has come to consider changing the rules as opposed to fighting a losing battle against the mainstream tides of safety and the need to fit in.

Although Captain Kirk is now a hero, as a cadet, his actions had people questioning his potential for leadership. While people debated the ethics of his tactics, Kirk went on to become an effective, high-ranking officer of the Starfleet Academy.

As we continue, we'll look at marketing from different perspectives. But nothing you read here will have been tackled AD nauseam[1] from other marketing texts. At some point, I realized that, much like the end product of most marketing campaigns, those texts have become vanilla, unmemorable, white noise, simply regurgitating old-school mentalities in shiny new packaging—something I have absolutely no interest in doing.

Together, we will rewrite all the rules and change the game.

---

[1] Get it? *Ad* nauseam? Puns are another MSV trait.

4: ARE YOU IN DANGER?

"Let me clue you in. I am not in danger, Skyler.
I AM the danger."

—Walter White

Heroes are so . . . predictable. I bet at one point or another you considered yourself the shining beacon of excellence in your industry. A hero would never say it out aloud, but you're so ahead of the curve you often wonder how your competitors can even tie their shoes in the morning. You truly believe it . . . hell, it's probably true, but why doesn't your bank account reflect it?

When the going gets tough, well . . . you know the rest. Like I said, predictable. But things keep getting tighter; shouldn't they be getting easier?

You either die a hero or live long enough to become a villain. Not ready to become a supervillain yet? Let's see how close to the dark side you already are. Count up how many of the phrases below have crept into your mind and keep score accordingly.

DEFCON 1 THOUGHTS: (1 Point Each)

1. New competitors? They'll never make it . . . but I wish 'em well.

2. There's a new **low-end market solution** but that's just for bottom-rung clients, not those I typically work with.

3. Might be time to "step on the gas" and really grow this company . . . but I have no idea how to do it.

4. Marketing doesn't work. Believe me, I've tried.

5. Maybe we should offer more services or add more features? That'll make everyone take notice for sure.

6. I may need to learn new skills to stay competitive . . . but I don't really want to.

7. I can't believe a prospect compared my services to that **low-end market solution**. That's like comparing apples to oranges!

8. I miss the good ole days.

9. Might be time to lower my prices to stay competitive.

10. I'm getting tired of responding to changes in my market. I used to define my market.

DEFCON 2 THOUGHTS: (2 Points Each)

11. The "new guys" are marketing . . . but those marketing agencies I hired in the past were buffoons and a waste of money.

12. What I've tried hasn't worked. I need a new approach. But I have enough on my plate trying to keep things afloat. FML.

13. That cheap **low-end market solution** is coming up more and more in conversations. I'm getting really tired of speaking about it.

14. We have plenty of differentiators that make us THE BEST . . . but these stupid clients don't seem to care about them!

15. This entire industry is going downhill . . . it's not just me.

16. I never considered an exit strategy before but maybe that's not a bad idea.

17. Downsizing is inevitable . . . I wonder how long I can fight it off?

18. We really need to update our website and increase our social media presence to let people know how different we are.

19. Welp, I updated my website and put pictures of our new, cool company swag on Facebook and no one liked it. WTF?!

20. Wait a minute . . . that shitty **low-end market solution** is getting a Super Bowl commercial?!

DEFCON 3 THOUGHTS: (3 Points Each)

21. I was at a party, and I noticed I felt a little empty whenever I described to people what I did for a living. I used to get a charge out of pounding my chest. What's going on? Maybe I'm just depressed.

22. Clients are starting to become more and more discerning. They are asking more questions but not the right ones! The clients are the problem. If I only had really educated clients that knew how good we really are. *That* would be a game changer.

23. Is this what disruption looks like? Where is my laptop? I need to google DISRUPTION.

24. Before I close the laptop, let me google my own company. Where the hell am I?! I used to be on page 1?! I'm on page

freakin' 8 of Google?!?!? I knew that marketing company I hired was useless.

25. I've given everything to this industry and what has it gotten me? Thanks for nothing.

26. Maybe downsizing isn't so bad. I'll become lean and mean. My experience and expertise could turn this place into a well-oiled machine unlike anywhere else.

27. I miss the passion and rush I got for solving client problems. Now it's like I work on a production line.

28. Went to another party. Someone asked me what I did for a living. I just changed the subject.

29. Everyone's talking about content creation. Maybe it's time to start my blog and share my expertise.

30. Writing is hard. Who else in the company can I pawn this "blog thing" off on? I don't have time for this!

DEFCON 4 THOUGHTS: (4 Points Each)

31. Screw it, it might be time to hire another marketing agency. This time I'll tell them exactly what I want so there is no debate as to deliverables. SEO? SEM? Social media? I don't understand any of this. I'll tell the agency I want all of it. What's the worst that can happen?

32. This marketing agency doesn't get the nuances of our industry . . . it's only been two weeks, but it may be time to make some bigger changes.

33. A key employee left us for one of the "new guys," probably because they have a Ping-Pong table. Huge mistake. There's no substance there. Good luck, pal. (He'll come crawling back.)

34. Look at that, the "new guys" got one 100 likes on their Instagram post about their Ping-Pong table.

35. Our company culture really needs a shot of adrenaline. Where's all the buzz we used to have?

36. Maybe we should get a Ping-Pong table?

37. Maybe I shouldn't have thrown that guy out of my office who wanted to talk about a merger five years ago. I'm nowhere near my peak valuation, but I wonder if he'd take my call?

38. I should really start attending an industry conference. It's a deductible vacation. Why not? Oh, profits are down, I can't afford to go to the conference, and it's halfway across the globe.

39. Oh, it's not so bad. Everyone's experiencing the same thing as me.

40. I swear, the next person that mentions that *low-end market solution* is getting punched in the throat.

SCORECARD:

0-10 points: You may be safe, only time will tell . . .

11-21 points: You've accepted that there is danger on the horizon and your guard is up.

22-32 points: Your guard is up and gloves are off, it's time to fight back. Kicking, scratching, biting—everything is legal in this scenario.

33-50+ points: Maybe you actually have punched someone in the throat for mentioning that low-end market solution. It's time to take this stuff seriously! Let's get to work.

5: ORIGIN STORY

"Flair is what marks the difference between artistry and mere competence."

**—William T. Riker, first officer
of the USS Enterprise in 2364**

Every superhero has an alter ego. Superman has Clark Kent. Batman has Bruce Wayne. The Green Goblin(s) walk among us as Harry and Norman Osborn. The alter ego is an outer shell that helps them move in the world more easily and shields the world from their true identity.

By contrast, every supervillain has an origin story—an inciting incident that rips the shell of normalcy away, birthing their contrasting perspective. It may be exposure to harmful radiation, a mishap during a late-night cryogenic research session, or the loss of a loved one at the hands of someone seen as "righteous."

For MSVs, it's that pivotal point in your career where you fully and clearly realize the insanity of your industry. It removes the shell that has protected you from the craziness of your world but has now become too small for your own vision. It has been inside of you waiting for you to unlock a powerful yet unpopular perspective. The day it is realized, crystalized, and formed into a personal "This Fucking Industry of Mine" story is the true origin story of your Marketing Supervillain.

The mild-mannered secret identities/alter egos do not strive for excellence, the spotlight, a big promotion, or a corner office. Their main reason for being is to throw others off the trail of their true intentions that lie beneath. They're bland by design.

Superman created mild-mannered reporter Clark Kent to help protect the ones he cared about. On the flip side, innocuous billionaire Bruce Wayne created Batman to protect the city. Which came first? The chicken or the egg? Is Tyler Durden the Fight Club-loving alter ego of Jack, or is Jack the alter ego of Tyler Durden? This debate will be saved for another, much nerdier book, but what I can tell you for sure is that in my early years, the life of a mild-mannered, under-the-radar "normie" was definitely the life for me, or so I thought. Inciting incidents are paramount in an origin story. They can be catalyzed by either an internal or external force. Mine was external and its name was Mr. Parisi, my junior high school art teacher.

Mr. Parisi must have belonged to some supervillainous legion of educators, as he was able to masterfully manipulate me and completely switch my way of thinking.

Much like the term supervillain, the word "manipulate" often comes with a negative connotation. The true definition, however, relates to the handling of situations in a highly skilled or masterful manner, and Mr. Parisi did just that with me.

It was roughly 11:00 a.m. and I was in my eighth-grade, fourth-period art class deliberately avoiding eye contact with anyone to maintain my "anonymity" and stay under the radar. The assignment was to pick a topic from a hat and begin drawing whatever came into your mind.

I got lucky. I reached into the hat and picked out a piece of paper that said "Fried Egg." I returned to my assigned seat along with the other rank and file and began my project. Nice and easy, no deep thought required; hell, I only needed a regular pencil and a yellow one.

I was progressing along on the best damn drawing of a fried egg you had ever seen. Mr. Parisi came by and, from over my shoulder, looked at my masterpiece. "Fried egg, huh?"

"*Yup!*" I replied, as I proudly reviewed my perfect yellow circle yolk surrounded by simple, off-white albumen. I nailed this project.

He reached down, picked up my masterpiece, and looked at it more closely. "Is this the first thing that came to mind?"

"*Yup!*" I replied. (Alter egos are not beings of many words.) He paused for a moment, then crumpled up my beautiful egg. While his scrambling of my masterpiece did not really upset me, the sound of crumpling paper caused everyone's eyes to lift off their art and look at me. Now, I was mortified. I wanted my egg back simply so I could crawl inside the shell and be invisible.

"What's the next thing that comes into your head?" he asked dismissively before moving on to another student.

I certainly wasn't going to raise a huff or create a scene, even though internally I felt somewhat double-crossed, doing what I was told only to have the bull's-eye moved after the fact. In my head, I was flipping over the art tables one by one and splashing paint all over the walls; in reality I just put my head down and began drawing and thinking. Nothing wrong here! Back to work, everyone.

The next thing that came to my mind for the term "Fried Egg" was that of an anthropomorphized egg nervously awaiting execution in the electric chair. I excitedly continued down this more enlightened creative path, deciding to include a government-mandated witness booth filled with other eggs. From behind the glass, some wept in sorrow and others looked on vengefully, for whatever atrocities prisoner 103945 had committed. I then sketched an egg with a black hooded mask standing by "The Switch." The Egg-secutioner.

"Dude! Check out what Wroblewski is doing," cried a passerby. Soon my fear was realized. I was the center of attention. As others gathered around, I expected to feel my blood pressure rise and my heart start to pound out of my chest, but the dread never set in. People were smiling and laughing. Some classmates who were "too cool for the room" and didn't want to join the masses directed their giggles onto me as if to say "what a weirdo." But you know what, I didn't mind it too much. It seemed like the beginnings of my brand had found me and, rather than hide from it, I chose to build upon it. This was the beginning of my origin story, a pivotal moment that defined me outside of the definition I had given myself.

While I was certainly not yet ready to completely accept this new loosely formed supervillain alter ego, much like the Riddler leaving clues from the shadows for Batman, I began to lean into this new brand that had emerged. To be honest, it gave me new life.

6: ORIGIN STORY PART 2 . . . GETTING WEIRDER

"Is it weird in here or is it just me?"
—Steven Wright

Here's the craziest thing: as I embodied my newly identified weirdness, it turned out it wasn't all that new. I realized that I always tended to lean into the more offbeat things in life. As a child, I wasn't educated on brand differentiation (who was?) and I wasn't deliberately trying to be a counterculture hipster. I was just built that way . . .weird.

Where other kids my age were collecting and trading baseball cards, I was the only one with a full and complete set of Garbage Pail Kids and Wacky Packages, a series of collectible stickers that parodied popular brands. My personal favorite was a take on L'eggs, the iconic pantyhose that came in an egg. The parody was *L'oggs*—pantyhose that made your legs look like two logs. Who wouldn't buy that?!

Like I said: I was just built weird.

25

In 1984, Michael Jackson, the King of Pop, fascinated the world. It seemed as if everyone I knew was transfixed on television's newest channel called MTV. It appeared that everyone waited with bated breath for his next music video to air—which, in my weird opinion, was all too often.

MJ's video "Beat It" opened with a gang member tapping his homie on the back, alerting him that it was time for action. It was overplayed, over-revered, and simply grated on my nerves. One day, I was watching the television with my cousin and, much to our chagrin, it looked as if "Beat It" was about to air for the umpteenth time that day. I got up to get a snack when my cousin shouted, "Hey, I never noticed that before!"

I turned around and looked. And then it happened, the coolest thing my nine-year-old eyes had ever witnessed.

This time, when the gang member slapped his buddy on the back, the coconspirator spit his coffee all over the bar. *Wait! What was going on? How had I previously missed that?* I hadn't, but my world completely changed. I now had a role model through which I could embrace what made me different, my "weirdness."

"Weird Al" Yankovic's since it's first mention masterful send-up, finish their dinners. juxtaposed the original video's serious tone and gang-violence visuals against the futility of trying to get kids to finish their dinner in "Eat It."

I took to Al's unique brand of music and entertainment and became a devout follower of everything weird and wonderful that he created. Ultimately Al, in all his creative weirdness, and in my opinion, genius, taught me my first invaluable lesson in differentiation.

After countless viewings of the "Eat It" video, I, along with a bunch of my friends, decided to let Al know how much we appreciated him. We handwrote and mailed him fan letters. (Email wasn't yet a thing.) As I got to the part of every fan letter where you close out with "I'm your biggest fan, I would love an autographed photo . . ." little Jesse James Wroblewski decided to disrupt the fan mail process.

Because I knew my audience, I closed my letter with a weird request: "If you have any lying around, I would love an autographed photo of . . . Joyce DeWitt." She was the actress who played Janet on the sitcom *Three's Company*.

It was clear, by his prompt response, Al didn't have any actual photos of her. He did, however, send a signed autographed photo of himself inscribed with "To Jesse, With Love, Joyce DeWitt."

More than 30 years later, I still love Al and everything he does. I proudly display my prized photo on my desk because, honestly, I just think it's funny. But Al also helped me realize differentiating myself in a crowded space is just as important as knowing my audience.

Someone before me had the courage to express his genius through his weirdness and, in doing so, he planted the seeds of differentiation in me at a very early age. So, Al, thank you.

By the way, most of my friends who used the generic sign-off are still waiting on their autographs.

7: WHAT EXACTLY IS "WRONG" WITH ME?

"My idea of an interesting person is someone who is quite proud of their seemingly abnormal life and turns their disadvantage into a career."

—John Waters

Adolescence amplifies a teenager's awkward quirks, yet mine felt a bit quirkier than those of my peers. I found myself seeking out, with increasing fervor, the more offbeat things in life. Lesser known and often polarizing brands, bands, movies and TV shows gave me much greater pleasure than what the populace had agreed upon. I soon found myself pledging my allegiance to underdog brands such as ECW wrestling, Troma Films, and underground metal and punk bands (as the hipsters would say: "Don't worry, you probably never heard of them.").

My passion for what I would call "my brands" grew at a feverish pace. While that was happening, I noticed an increasing disdain for other brands that did not align with my incredibly heightened, finely tuned, sommelier-like sensibilities for pop culture or brands I pledged allegiance to. Like a sports fan with two home teams, you couldn't call yourself a die-hard fan of the Yankees without truly hating the Mets.

In my "elevated" opinion, if you didn't watch the gritty and ultrarealistic matches of ECW wrestling but instead only tuned in to its mainstream competitors, you clearly weren't a true wrestling fan. If you didn't like metal music such as Pantera, you were a sellout or a sheep. Thinking back, I was probably a nightmare to be around. Some might be kind enough to categorize my character as normal, teenage rebellion, but I certainly had a unique way of processing the world and it didn't really make sense to me until I started dating.

When you're dating as a teenager, in order to see if you are truly a someone, you get right down to the "real" issues in life. You know, the hard-hitting deal-breakers such as "What's your favorite movie?" or "What type of music do you listen to?" All of the girls I dated would ultimately say (in a tone and cadence reminiscent of Ben Stein taking attendance during *Ferris Bueller's Day Off*) "Oh, I like whatever's on the radio" or "I'm easy, I can listen to country or rap, it's all good." I felt like I had entered a *Sesame Street* skit with the two alien Yip-Yips. "Yip yip yip yip yip." Once I heard their responses, I knew the relationship was doomed.

At the time, I intolerantly chalked it up to their lack of refined taste. In turn, they would criticize me by asking why I simply couldn't just like one thing without hating another. They'd exclaim, "It's the nineties! It's an amazing time in music to just be a fan." I wasn't buying it.

I felt that if you were a person who simply liked everything, it meant you truly loved nothing. I couldn't understand how others could exist without that fire in their belly for a particular position. Like-minded friends and I would joke that these passionless, unpolarized people would go home after work and, much like an emotionless android, sit in a chair, staring at the wall until they were powered back up in time for work. To boot, they were perfectly fine with a numbingly mundane existence.

But like Sarah Connor in *Terminator 2*, I was desperately trying to stop my seemingly unavoidable, predestined, dystopian future. It was a doomed fate, with a milquetoast wife and a den whose walls had meaningless, department store artwork like LIVE LOVE LAUGH. I wanted so much more, and I tried anything I could to label that feeling. When I felt a visceral connection with a brand, I had the undeniable urge to throw up my hands in the devil-horns gesture.

When you are truly committed (some might even call it "obsessed"), you find the answers to your questions in the most unexpected places. For me, it was in a martial arts dojo. In most martial arts styles, there are attack moves that not only require all of your focus and energy but an additional shout which helps focus your power. This short shout is called a *kiai*. If you've ever seen a martial arts movie, you've no doubt witnessed a stereotypical "HI-YA!" yell with a karate chop or an "EEE-YAH!" with a kick.

Regardless of what the actual *kiai* sounded like, I noticed it was usually associated with the same sneering face I made when I threw up the devil horns. I realized that I was indeed putting my everything into these brands I loved.

That was a clue. I continued to dig until I finally found it. While English language did not have a word for it, Japanese actually did!

おたく.

For those of you who do not read Japanese, those kanji (the Japanese lettering) are pronounced *otaku*.

Otaku is "the space between a hobby and an obsession." For me, it expressed my impassioned connection with a brand that was so authentic and powerful that I would actually will that brand to succeed. In many cases, my brand allegiance was so strong that I would be willing to get a tattoo of their logo, if they asked.

Once I realized that *otaku* existed, I wanted to find a way to manufacture it. What if I could take the feeling I had for *my brands* and create it for the customers of my *clients'* products and services? As an agency, I'd have lightning in a bottle.

Creating calls to action and chasing high click-through rates like everyone else was boring. Anyone could figure that out! At this point in our journey, I'm hoping you can now predict what happens when you chase the same goals as everyone else in your field.

I wanted to take on new frontiers and bigger challenges. I wanted to do the impossible, all of the time. I wanted to take brands to cult status and create an almost religious allegiance. I wanted to help companies to connect so authentically with their demographic that their followers would get a tattoo of the brand logo on their body.

8: THE DREADED "C WORD"

"Everything popular is wrong."
—Oscar Wilde

The nineties were a weird time for film. The action genre was hot, so naturally, Hollywood execs wanted to milk every dollar out of the demand by offering a never-ending supply of slight twists on a proven formula. Right before audiences were completely beaten down and exhausted with the premise, Warner Bros. snuck in one final blockbuster. A movie titled *Twister* pitted a ragtag group of lovable storm chasers against an evil corporate-funded conglomerate on a quest to capture lifesaving tornado data.

One of *Twister's* most ridiculous scenes (of which there are many!), the lovable hero team is gathered for breakfast, telling war stories of their encounters with tornadoes of different Fujita (F) forces. They all chime in about their experiences with F-2s, F-3s, and F-4s when a reporter utters the question "Is there an F-5?" Abruptly, the room goes silent. You can hear forks tinkling on plates, people swallowing, as everyone's eyes slowly rise from their meals, appalled at what they just heard. The group leader, played Scott Thomson's character says this (not Bill Paxton's) by the great Bill Paxton, exclaims that an F-5 was as powerful as "The Finger of God," which could destroy anything it touched. (Heroes are so nerdy and overly dramatic.)

For business owners, while this word may or may not be immediately apparent to them, it should be. Familiarizing yourself with your enemy is the key to victory on the battlefield. This archnemesis to any business owner could indeed wipe out your business much like The Finger of God would do to a landscape. It's the dreaded Cword.

I'm speaking about **COMMODITIZATION**.

What Does Becoming Commoditized Actually Mean?

If you haven't already dropped your fork in sheer terror, swallow that last bite of breakfast and let's shed some needed light on the subject. **A business becomes commoditized when its unique feature or benefit can easily be replaced by other competitors in the marketplace**. Sure, we know, your brand is different . . . and so is your competitor. You use better materials and more skilled providers . . . the same with your competitor. When, in the eyes of the consumer, there is no discernable difference between product choices, their decision becomes solely driven by price.

Hollywood execs have the luxury and the budget to differentiate a commoditized plot (such as a disaster movie) by replacing an erupting volcano (*Dante's Peak*) with a menacing tornado (*Twister*).

The force of commoditization pulls once-proud business owners and brand developers from a place of fulfillment and value into a race to the bottom. In order to compete at the lowest possible price, they have to cut corners, inevitably resulting in a cut in quality. It's a terrible position in which no businessperson with an ounce of ingenuity or pride would ever want to be.

Can It Happen to You?

Without a shadow of a doubt! Given a long enough timeline, everything will eventually become a commodity. Accelerated by the internet, consumers now have an "explosion of choice," a term marketing thought leader Seth Godin coined in his book, *The Purple Cow.* He states, "As the number of choices on the market for a product or service increases, the likelihood of becoming commoditized increases as well."

As more competitors—and more options—enter the market, constant improvement of existing products and services will no longer suffice. With rare exceptions, we are all susceptible to commoditization. How do I know? Because it happened to me! If it can happen to a supervillain like me, no one is safe.

My Brush with Disaster

When I was running and scaling my own marketing agency, I was following a well-trodden path: Perfect your skill set, grow a team of key expert players, build an impressive headquarters, and expand your service offerings. Lots of risk and hard work, sure, but eventually you got to play with the big boys.

Alas, similar to an F-5, COVID came along and disrupted everything for me. My impressive headquarters, with all of its insanely talented people who perfectly gelled to create the most positive collective energy I've ever experienced in my 25-year career, was swept away into the world of remote "team" work.

All my key differentiators were abruptly relegated to a Zoom box. Corporate clients who previously turned up their noses at any agency without a dedicated, on-site team toiling away on their projects no longer minded (not that they had a choice). In the past, I'd cringe at the thought of damaging my brand if a team member had to work from home and dial into a meeting. What if a dog barked? Or a child was heard in the background? Or even worse, what if they suspected someone was a hired gun and not a dedicated salaried employee, an outlier who hadn't fully adopted our amazing corporate culture and routines?

With my finely tuned brand in jeopardy, my office closed, I put pinball machines and Ping-Pong tables in storage; most of my differentiating factors had been removed. I, like the rest of the world, had been relegated to doing business (prospecting, team meetings, project management, creative sessions, etc.) in my tiny Zoom room. My team offerings were not as attractive as they once were, and companies were willing to give solopreneurs with limited infrastructure and off-shore options another look. The same people who demanded professional perfection were now completely fine meeting with others in their pajamas like a big, happy corporate sleepover party.

There were simply too many choices in the market to maintain the same level of competitiveness as before. My business had become commoditized.

I had to decide: Should I close up shop? Put on a white belt and start over? Learn how to dominate a completely new landscape? Or stick to my guns and hope to survive the changing tide long enough to eke out a retirement before it all goes kaput? Evolve or die?

I chose the former.

It was time to get back into my MSV lair, plan a resurrection in the face of disruption, and document all of my findings to share with a select few. (Yes, that's you!)

My MSV lair was an aboveground bunker created from a shipping container I had delivered to my backyard. I needed an office outside of my home office to gain some level of structure in my work-life balance. Or maybe I just wanted to build a badass supervillain lair with my newfound pandemic-sponsored free time. Probably a mix of both.

The search for the Kryptonite that could stop commoditization in its tracks and make me Future-Proof began.

I found it.

I trademarked it.

I named it.

I shall call you . . . Decommodization™.

This effing industry of mine was in for a revolution.

9: THE FIRST MARKETING SUPERVILLAIN

*"Heroes see danger and attack it head-on
while villains see the madness in the world and
reshape it to their will."*

—Jeff Mach

It was 1500 BCE and a Sumerian named Temen was celebrating his prosperous future. Temen was a brick merchant, and fortune shone down upon him when a rudimentary method of mass production had improved, allowing Temen to create and sell more bricks than ever before. The world was his oyster. His celebratory mood, however, was quickly dashed.

At his Mesopotamian marketplace, Temen began noticing trends. This new mass-producing method was not exclusive to his industry. The concept began spilling into other verticals: ceramics, sails, and wheels. With the availability of more products, his customers now had more choices. To make matters worse, the barrier of entry to becoming a brick merchant was significantly lower. His unique skill, passed down from generation to generation, was now easily replicable.

Commoditization was starting to turn Temen into a nobody.

Temen knew trouble was ahead and devised a plan. His knee-jerk reaction was to attack the threat head-on. *Maybe I could hire some thugs to trash every other competitor's operation,* he mused. It was tempting, but he knew it wasn't sustainable. He needed a way to sway the masses into buying his goods instead of his new competitors'. While history tells us that the ancient Sumerians had always been a culture of high innovation, Temen's customers were not highly educated. His prospects were busy people. They paid no mind to the particular qualities he placed on his bricks, compared to the new options in the marketplace.

Temen knew that trying to educate his customers on every aspect of brick manufacturing and quality was a long and tiresome way of shaping their decisions. If only there was a simpler way of controlling their decisions.

After some long nights of pondering, Temen came up with his solution. He'd place a simple mark on his bricks to let customers know who made them and where they could return them should they run into any problems. It was a subtle way to let uneducated brick buyers know that Temen was unwavering in his commitment to his product.

This genius tactic caught on, and as a result, consumer confidence immediately increased, as did sales. Not only had Temen differentiated his product, but he had created such a buzz in his "mark-eting" that he was able to charge a premium. Chalk up another business innovation to the Mesopotamians: the concept of marketing.

Merchants began attempting to build trust and goodwill by marking their products, their cattle and even their slaves, with a stamp. Sometimes the only way to make your mark permanent on a steer or even a person was with the use of a branding iron, thus the term "brand" was born and the world was introduced to logos.

I must admit, I find Temen to be a bit of a genius. You see, many commoditized brands will try to educate their customers on why their product/service is better than their competitors'. Yet it's a rare customer that buys the steak and not the sizzle. Your job as a marketer is to sell, not to educate. Temen never got into the education game; he instead focused on marketing, which then naturally led to branding.

This, however, is where most marketers and marketing agencies stop. They take part in an arms race of branding and marketing, using the same exact tools their competitors are using. Create a nice-looking logo, and then so do your competitors. Start an AdWords campaign with some great keywords, and (or then) your competitors do the same, with the same keywords, making this campaign less effective and more costly as each new competitor enters the game to bid on your precious keywords. Search Engine Optimization (SEO) is the same type of zero-sum game; stay at it long enough and someone will pitch you on how they know some magic keywords that the competitors haven't yet thought of.

When all is said and done, and your strategy and campaigns are netting negative returns, there is only one answer: time for the great REBRAND! And the cycle starts all over again. It's a nice little racket if you are a marketer for hire. (I promise I won't blow your cover on the never-ending race of continuously upselling clients and making boatloads of cash.)

The problem is that marketing, then branding, is just the start of this new evolution. The next steps, for all forward-looking brands, needs to be *Decommoditization*™.

10: THE ONLY WEAPON YOU NEED

Duck and Cover!

—Bert the Turtle

For those of you reading this who are under the age of forty, *Duck and Cover* was an educational film from the 1950s and 1960s, seen by over fifty million schoolchildren. Its purpose, believe it or not, was to teach them what to do in the event of a nuclear explosion.

During the Atomic Age, Bert the Turtle was an American cartoon who explained to these doomed youngsters that simply ducking under their school desks and covering their heads would shield them from an enemy attack of a 60-megaton atomic explosion.

Looking back, the advice is laughable. But following the advice of SMM, SEO and PPC "experts" is equally laughable, and the doom of your business's commoditization is also inevitable.

WHAT SHOULD YOU DO?

Listen to Bert the Turtle and just duck and cover?

Sure, if you're looking for a quick and guaranteed demise.

To be honest, I feel as if I am living in the '50s again. Well over 50 years from now, all of the mainstream-published content on how to fight off commoditization will be mocked just as hard, proven to be just as useless as that cartoon turtle's battle cry.

A simple Google search shows results from notable respected outlets, such as *Forbes*, claiming the answer is to simply offer unparalleled customer service, bundle your services, and do a better job of educating your clients.

While you're at it, don't forget to bring along your favorite blankie to protect you from potential radiation fallout from a megaton blast.

This information is just as useless.

As a business owner or brand developer, you know by now that commoditization is equivalent to the apocalypse and it needs to be put in check. But how?

Maybe you've read all the books on "differentiation" and "unique sales propositions" (USPs). Almost all of them toss these two buzz phrases around like confetti on New Year's Eve. They'll convince you it's as easy as a walk in the park. All you have to do is drill down and discover your true, authentic differentiator or that of your clients.

After you've done that, they'll tell you to take that incredibly unique thing about your company and distill it to its core messaging and convey it to the masses. Simple, right? Wrong.

Differentiation is the ultimate weapon in a marketer's arsenal. However, the word is so misused and misunderstood that a truly differentiated brand has become rarer than a decent sequel to *The Matrix* movies.

Differentiation is the atomic bomb that can blow your industry apart and leave you standing as the sole victor, but it is complex and difficult. Lucky for you, there's a process for, it and I call it: Decommoditization.

Let's get to work.

11: I DON'T WANT TO RETIRE WITHOUT ANY SCARS

"I want you to hit me as hard as you can."

—Tyler Durden, Fight Club

Fight Club is one of my all-time favorite movies. Even though it's fiction, I love the analogy it allows me to draw for business and the problem with making difficult, uncomfortable changes.

(Fair warning: the statute of limitations is over and there are some spoilers coming in this chapter.)

In *Fight Club*, the main character, whom we'll call Jack, is asked by a new friend, Tyler Durden, to hit him as hard as he can. Late one night, in a dimly lit parking lot, Jack obliges with a right hook to Tyler's left ear . . . and Fight Club is born.

On that fateful night, when Jack punched Tyler Durden, Jack was actually punching himself. Tyler Durden was Jack's alter ego.

But lest you forget, the first rule of Fight Club is that WE DO NOT TALK ABOUT FIGHT CLUB.

So why are we breaking the first rule? More importantly, how does this apply to your business?

As business owners, doing something even slightly outside of the norm to achieve market differentiation may seem terrifying. Change is hard and uncomfortable, but you need to prepare yourself for it, because in order to consistently compete in the fight in your industry, it is also inevitable. It may even hurt . . . like punching yourself in the face. Am I suggesting you do that? No. Well, maybe yes, but . . . *no*. And perhaps, just like Jack's first fight on that fateful night, no one will even pay attention to you, or the few who do may simply shrug you off as a crazy person.

But that label didn't stop Jack. He felt something authentic inside and kept coming back night after night to do what made him feel alive, to do what he felt was right. And because he wasn't afraid to follow his inner voice, other people got it and followed the path he had the courage to pave. Crowds formed and ultimately *Fight Club* became a global entity. The fact is, being true to your own authenticity takes courage and discomfort. Many business owners shy away from this.

Jack leaned into the discomfort of doing something outside of the norm. His ability to be courageously authentic and follow his gut was so powerful that others began talking about him and Fight Club. He became a brand not by simply talking about Fight Club, but by embodying all that Fight Club was.

Let's face it: in today's business environment, social media and business are so intertwined that business owners feel the pressure to continuously post "look at me" messages. How incredible would it be to put out substance for your brand that's so authentic and so powerful that others can't help but talk about it and share it for you?

Differentiation may seem scary and even dangerous, but who wants to retire without any scars or war stories? Let's dive in and discover what truly makes you different. The first step is authenticity.

12: THE SPOOKY/GENIUS WAY ABC DECOMMODITIZED THE AMERICAN FAMILY

"Sic Gorgiamus Allos Subjectatos Nunc"

—Addams Family Crest: We Will Gladly Feast On Those Who Would Subdue Us

In television, the American sitcom is one of the biggest commodities. Networks, however, continue to crank out the same content in the hopes of somehow striking a chord with the viewing audience. They think that by changing only a small ingredient here and there, they can make it "different."

In 1964, ABC took a chance and aired something truly unique, a show that purposely flipped the script and challenged everything the audience knew about the typical American family. The show spawned a character so perfectly differentiated, he quickly became one of my idols.

When the sky was blue, he called it gloomy. When it was dark and stormy, he was packing for the beach. Rain—well, rain was just heavenly.

Independently wealthy, gorgeous wife, tight-knit family, and hobbies galore. Who had it better than Gomez Addams?

Gomez had all the makings of a supervillain. He was an outlier in a big creepy house who was not only different physically but also philosophically and fundamentally unlike anyone else.

Yet Gomez relentlessly welcomed every person of every lifestyle with open arms, even when they were outright opposed to his— which almost always happened. His graciousness never felt forced, underhanded, or like pandering because Gomez was authentic—a key ingredient in being a differentiator.

Gomez's superpower was inspiring authenticity. He gave courage to other outliers to differentiate themselves in the pursuit of success.

With the first U.S. sitcom starting in 1926, we are approaching a century of this style of entertainment. Thousands upon thousands of characters later, it's Gomez and his family of differentiators that are continually brought back from the dead in the form of feature films, Broadway musicals, animated series, video games, and even a Netflix series.

Why? I think it's because as outlandish as they seem to be, there is at least a little bit of the Addamses in every one of us. Often, we hide what makes us different for fear of criticism and rejection, but Gomez leaned into his differentiating characteristics because he only knew how to live his life from a place of authenticity. And his commitment to doing so sparked a fire in each one of us to do the same.

Deep down, you're either rooting for the differentiator or you're wanting, waiting, or destined to become one.

13: AUTHENTICITY FIRST!

> "I used to think the worst thing in life was to end up all alone. It's not. The worst thing in life is ending up with people who make you feel all alone."
>
> **—Robin Williams (World's Greatest Dad)**

If you are going to achieve world domination (or for you MSVs with a less ambitious goal, industry domination), I would strongly suggest you start from a place of—you guessed it—authenticity.

Certainly, you can choose many starting points on your path to becoming the supreme ruler of your industry. Personally, I've tried approaching the task from an economical angle. Identify a market in need with some capital to spend. Match it up with an ingenious plot or product to soothe said need.

I've also tried the other, more egotistical approach (which admittedly I realized was ass-backward): Invent something from scratch, figure out who needs it most, and then take on the tremendously larger challenge of working out how the hell I'm going to reach those potential customers.

Through trial and error, reading countless books on every imaginable topic, and speaking with more people than any introvert would imagine doing, I found that when your own authenticity aligns with your positioning in your marketplace, your chances of success increase exponentially. Who wouldn't want such a leg up on the quickest path to success? So let's adjust your headspace into thinking like a true MSV. Your genius mindset is precious. Each minute you devote to an entrepreneurial dead end puts you a few steps behind the competition.

As I continued my inner search to become professionally authentic, I realized my largest and most glaring problem. I fell into the career trap of being a generalist. It was most apparent when friends, family, and clients, who knew I worked in the tech world, would come to me to fix their nonfunctioning desktops, even though my firm was a marketing and advertising one! And, like an idiot, I'd try to solve those problems. *Maybe*, I thought, *this is something I could roll into our existing suite of services. Maybe I'll turn my agency into a one-stop shop for anything involving a keyboard and mouse.* This mentality was reflected in how I took on clients: if you had a pulse and a bank account, you were fair game.

One-stop shopping seemed like a worthy goal and potential differentiator . . . but it wasn't. There's a reason big-box department stores are crumbling before our eyes and farmers' markets are proliferating.

Trying to be everything to everyone quickly made me nothing to anyone. I wasn't known for truly being the best at anything. When someone has a genuine, life-threatening business problem, they seek out a specialist—not the guy or agency that kindasorta did it all.

I began my quest for reinvention. I jumped on this search with the enthusiasm of a (pre-bingeable) *Breaking Bad* fan excited to see how Walter White was going to get himself out of the mess he had gotten himself into the previous week.

All I needed to do was "niche down." (At least that's what the cornucopia of books purported. Simply choose a single industry or a single service to focus on. Then choose a segment of that industry or service and finally a micro segment of said industry and service and "Voila," you have become a specialist in a "niche" and success will be giveth onto you.) Simple! I tirelessly sought out a perfect vertical that was worthy of 100% of my marketing and creative prowess. A vertical that was ripe with cash flow. A vertical that wasn't overly saturated with competitors. A vertical with a clear problem that needed to be solved.

It was as if a perfect storm was circulating directly above Dr. Frankenstein's castle and I, with my hand on the lever, yanked it down and quite literally caught lightning in a bottle. The vertical I had identified was so starved for marketing solutions they were spending upwards of a quarter of a million dollars *per month* on PPC ads just to stay relevant in their respective conversations. Bingo, now I was ready. I had my niche, it was ripe for the picking, and my team of minions was highly skilled and ready to deliver. What could go wrong?

Plenty.

I missed one vital checkbox. In all fairness, it was easy to miss because it wasn't on the checklist provided by all of the "how-to position yourself" articles and books in circulation. (Yes, true supervillains have to invent *everything*.) The box they had missed was Authenticity. When it came right down to it, my decision for specializing my agency wasn't authentic to me, and that lack of authenticity oozed out of my marketing pores when I worked with a client. Like a child or animal who can instinctively sense fear and insecurity, so did my clients.

My new agency checked all of the logical boxes but none of the emotional ones. When it came right down to it, I had no interest in writing a heartfelt book on the vertical I had chosen. Hell, writing a single *blog post* on the subject was tedious, unfulfilling homework. Like any good schoolchild, I put it off until I had absolutely nothing else on my to-do list and had to face the reality that it was time to sit and write.

In a 2019 agency boot camp with positioning expert Blair Enns, he suggested envisioning yourself about to be introduced at a world-renowned keynote. The emcee says, "Ladies and gentlemen, today we are lucky enough to be joined by the world's leading authority on [insert your specialty]. Please welcome [insert your name]!" Once you figure out that introduction, you're set on your positioning.

Sadly, I did not read Blair's nugget of genius until after I had sunk thousands of dollars and countless hours of brainpower into my venture. I didn't want to put in the deep work on something I wasn't personally passionate about.

If you are on a quest for positioning, authenticity *must* come first. The authenticity that is part of my genetic makeup is decommoditization.

Everything I do, from the way I dress to how I stage my office. It's how I experience my world. It permeates every cell of my being . . .

To truly be the best in the world, what you do must be woven into your DNA. Differentiation serves as a lens to everything I see and hear. What lessons on differentiation can be learned from watching my favorite movie? How did last night's episode of *Monday Night Raw* relate to a book on differentiating I was reading? How many ways has my new favorite rapper essentially decommoditized himself in a saturated landscape? Decommoditize, decommoditize,

decommoditize. Obsessive, you might ask? Absolutely. And I would also add, necessary. I challenge you to name me one person who has achieved an exalted level of success who hasn't been obsessive. Opportunities are abundant at the crossroads of obsession and awareness.

Here's a simple fact: no supervillain has ever stood upon their empire slamming down their fist and maniacally laughing in triumph for being the best in the world while sacrificing themself for something they *kindasorta* believed in.

PART II

THE HOW:

14: THE UNIVERSE OF DIFFERENTIATION

*"I'll sell my invention so that
everyone can be superheroes.
And with everyone super . . . no one will be."*

—Syndrome, The Incredibles

If the goal of positioning and differentiation is to be unlike anything that exists or has ever existed in the universe, it would seem that creating a procedure to achieve such a lofty feat would be impossible.

But in marketing supervillainy, we live to do the impossible. We thrive on the claims of others who say, "That can't be done," or "No one ever tried that before," or my favorite: "That really SHOULDN'T be done."

I proudly present to you the Universe of Differentiation.

I've taken the top 12 methods of differentiation utilized by successful brands of all sizes, some who populate the Fortune 500 list and some who dominate their local market. I gave each of these differentiation methods its own planet within the universe.

On many planets there live differentiated citizens who could easily blend in with the citizens of other differentiated planets, as there is a fine thread of connectivity across the entire universe of differentiation. You may look at a brand claiming to be the oldest in their vertical. That brand is using three differentiators: *timing*, *heritage*, and its *definitive* status as the oldest.

This does not make the method of differentiation any less powerful; it merely opens ideas as to how these tactics of decommoditization can be combined for an even more powerful result. Imagine a mad scientist hard at work in front of a shelf of powerful chemicals. While each bubbling and roiling beaker is powerful on its own, a combination of the fluids by a mastermind and skilled hand can create something truly earth-shattering.

The Universe of Differentiation consists of the following planets:

- Definitives
- Approachable Distinction
- Exclusivity & Scarcity
- Personification
- Lifestyle
- Heritage
- Process
- Niching Down
- Repositioning the Category
- Timing
- Cause Alignment
- Byproduct

Your first step in conquering this universe is reconnaissance. Get to know each planet and its inhabitants thoroughly. In the next 12 chapters, we'll visit these planets one by one. We'll analyze their environments and observe a common persona or two of brands who live there. Once you know the lay of the land, we can begin the process of choosing the juiciest and most profitable areas of opportunity on our way to taking over the galaxy.

15: PLANET ONE: THE USE OF DEFINITIVES

"Every hospital claims to have the best doctor in the galaxy. It's like those pizza places that claim to have the best pizza in the world. What—Do you think they have pizza contests?"

—Rick Sanchez, Rick & Morty

The first stop on our tour of the Universe of Differentiation is the planet DEFINITIVE.

I'm certain you've experienced differentiation through definitives. We sell *the most* hamburgers. Our prices are *the lowest*. If you want *the safest* automobile, look no further than us.

You've heard these differentiators so much that they've almost completely lost the power to truly differentiate a brand. This style of differentiation has become commoditized in its own right. It has become the white noise of differentiation.

When it comes to the bottom line, doesn't everyone think they are the best? Aside from Avis's "When you're only No. 2, you try harder" ad campaign, I can't recall anyone going to market promoting their averageness.

I have to admit that I've been guilty of this. I thought bringing my A game at all times was the only way to excel. While this mentality is how I'm wired, it may not be the only way to win.

This "hardwired-to-win" mentality actually helped me win a global website design contest in the early years of my career. The prize itself actually helped change my perspective on business and how diverse the power of differentiation via definitives could be.

That prize? I got to live with "The Most Hated Band in the World," the Insane Clown Posse (ICP).

Sure, ICP (the brainchild of Violent J and Shaggy 2 Dope) has now become ingrained in pop culture and, as a result, is an easy target of memes, the butt of jokes, and even parodied on *Saturday Night Live*. To most, that would be a tremendous detriment. However, very early in my professional career, these two high school dropouts, who made their living dressed as clowns, opened my eyes on business and differentiation.

I was so enamored by their culture that I actually entered and won a website design contest run by their record company, garnering the chance to spend a weekend with them at their Detroit home. More on this later.

The band's outlandishness is what initially drew me to them. Even if you haven't seen their outrageous physical appearances, listened to their music, or viewed their crazy onstage antics, simply hearing their name should let you know how outside of the mainstream they are . . . Insane Clown Posse. What else could you possibly conclude?

ICP knew its brand and they leaned into it . . . hard. We're not, however, focusing on these two crazy clowns because of their outlandishness. To reiterate a common misconception about differentiation, being wild and outlandish is not the only way to distinguish yourself in a crowded market. Not by a long shot. They differentiated themselves through a *definitive*.

Winning the website design contest landed me at ICP's independently owned e-commerce warehouse of multimillion-dollar inventory. I had a tour of ICP's private recording studio. While I conversed with the band, they admitted they were well aware they couldn't sing. My A-game wiring started to short out. How the hell was all this possible? How do you successfully market crap?

ICP was massively successful by almost deliberately not being the best. They actually leaned into their greatest asset . . . that they may in fact be some of the worst rappers in the world. That was their differentiator.

I began to wonder how I would market my company if I truly felt I simply wasn't the best at what I did. Did any other brands use counterintuitive differentiation to market themselves? And as I dug deeper, I realized this tactic was everywhere!

Other businesses knew this secret as well. The owners of the Oak Door Steakhouse knew they were never going to sell more hamburgers than McDonald's nor, could they ever compete on price. Not the biggest, not the cheapest, but still wanted to be included in the burger conversation. They went the opposite direction and now sell the world's most expensive hamburger coming in at almost $1,000. The **most expensive** was their differentiator.

Pappy Van Winkle continues to tout how rare their bourbon is and leans on how little of it they actually sell to the public. **The rarest**, a wonderful differentiator.

Who likes things to be tough or have obstacles in their life? Apparently lots of fitness enthusiasts do, as "Eco Race" makes a killing by marketing themselves as the world's toughest race. And

"Tough Mudder"? Well, they have the "Best Obstacles in The World." **The Toughest**.

Dangerously sour? Atomic Waste Candy has laid claim to that title. **The Sourest.**

In business, there are things we can't control. You can't always be the biggest in your market; you may not have the best or the highest-quality products. Maybe J.D. Power and Associates keep snubbing you at their awards ceremony.

A little differentiation can go a long way, but it doesn't always have to come from an expected place. Who are you in your marketplace? The ugliest? The largest? The meanest? The hardest to get to? Your differentiator is there. You just have to define it, lean into it, and take your brand out of the closet of commoditization.

Don't take my word for it. Take it from "The Most Hated Band in the World."

16: PLANET TWO: APPROACHABLE DISTINCTION

"I'd like to be more approachable, not less weird."

—Chloë Sevigny

There's a world of supervillainy and then there is a world of much greater, almost unspeakable evil. This place is wherever in the world our desktop printers come from. To quote the famous online comic *The Oatmeal*, "Printers have been sent here from hell."

We live in a world where we get a push notification that clearly explains the situation when your cat uses their robot litter box and has finally maxed out its poop capacity. When there is something wrong with your printer, however, it spits out the message **"err:X8752341 tray 1"** on a crappy LCD screen and you have to press one of two completely nondescript buttons until it finally goes away.

One can only assume there is a secret printer ink cartel hidden away in some part of the remote world lighting cigars with one-hundred-dollar bills as they laugh at us for paying insane prices for their ink, which I'm pretty sure is the same stuff inside the pen that I got for free from my dentist.

Simply put, printers are unapproachable. They are not intuitive, they're ugly, and they die at the most inopportune times without warning. Yet for some ungodly reason, these machines refuse to evolve. They suck just as much now as they did in 1995. And the marketing? That sucks too.

No one ever just wanders into the printer aisle to window-shop. That is because all desktop printer marketing is terrible.

It boggles my mind that not a single manufacturer out there has taken the differentiating strategy of making their product undeniably approachable.

Apple knew this when it entered the portable music marketplace. MP3? AIFF? WAV? What audio format is best? What about bit rate? What about storage space? Who was going to toss their perfectly reliable Walkman for a new technology if a research assignment came along with the process?

Apple's genius quelled all those fears; it went to great lengths to make their new device, the iPod, extremely approachable. They helped the savvy, curious consumer begin conversations about the product in a snap. As for the non-savvy consumer? Apple knew that the hardest question the company wanted to be asked about this incredible technological advancement was if they wanted one in white, blue, black, or pink.

Apple, both figuratively and literally, sanded off all of the rough edges, wrapped an MP3 player in plastic, and gave it a shiny, colorful paint job. They marketed their newly minted iPod with simple silhouettes of people dancing on bright colorful backgrounds to upbeat, popular music. The approachability of the go-to-market strategy replaced the need of research, white papers, online reviews, and watching product comparison videos with the warm feeling of being able to handle this technological jump as a consumer.

Meanwhile, back in the desktop printer aisle, you are faced with laser versus inkjet, pages per minute, ink sustainability, duplexing, collating, network-enabled or LAN, color or black and white, mobile printing, and warranties.

Approachability is about making people feel comfortable. It's about reducing the anxieties that surround both the purchasing and the use of your product or service.

Best of all, it's a method of differentiation that can organically be combined with other differentiation strategies.

17: PLANET THREE: EXCLUSIVITY & SCARCITY

"No one goes there anymore, it's too crowded."

—Yogi Berra

The textbook definition of our previous method of differentiation, approachability, is: *the quality of being easy to deal with or access.* The method of differentiation in this chapter is the polar opposite. We're going to raise the drawbridges and bomb the roads to our tiny island, making it truly excluded from the mainland. Welcome to the island of *exclusivity branding.*

The year is 1999. I was about a year into my career as a web designer, naively chasing any gig I could find. This naivete landed me in a meeting across from two men who were involved in organized crime. Needless to say, I survived the meeting conducted by actual villains and was able to turn down the deal after fully realizing what I had almost gotten myself into. This was my first contact with this type of method of differentiation and the story of the closest I ever came to building a website for the Mafia.

The meeting in question was with an existing client who had an e-commerce website dedicated to hair care products. The two "guests" at the meeting were explaining how they had developed a method of obtaining very sought-after hair care products previously restricted for sale to only high-end salons. The availability of these exclusive products would clearly make my client's website truly differentiated.

Unbeknownst to me, being at the sunrise of my career, the same exact manufacturers of everyday hair care products for the common man and woman also create "ultra-high-end versions" of these same products, aimed at an entirely different market.

Where the original products and packaging were overloaded with graphics, features, benefits, and explanations of their ingredients, these other higher-end packages were deliberately minimal in design. A sleek logo, some FDA-required verbiage on the back, and that was it. If you hadn't come across them in the environment of a luxury salon, you may have been perplexed as to whether the contents of the bottle should be rubbed into your hair or squeezed onto your hot dogs at your next BBQ.

Some portion of this unapproachable exclusivity was created through intimidation. I liken it to walking into a luxury car dealership and asking the price of the car. If you're there looking to buy a car, you won't dare ask a salesman for the price! Same thing at high-end salons. A customer would feel hesitant to ask a question of the "elevated experts" working within the salon. These customers didn't want to appear silly, naive, or dare I say, "cheap." If the manufacturers didn't have to tout the product's quality on the bottle, their confidence in its abilities must make it head and shoulders above the rest (puns!).

Doubling down on this concept, this industry created a covert plot to keep their products off the shelves of discount stores like Walmart and, most importantly, off of websites like the one owned by my client. Experiencing this particular brand in these places would no doubt diminish the exclusivity and scarcity of the formula and thus decrease the perceived value of the product.

To accomplish this effect, there is a hidden, customized serial number printed on each SKU. Each salon had a unique serial number assigned to it, in the last place anyone would look: on the inside of the bottle! Should some bottles of the prized potions make their way onto a store shelf deemed unworthy by the manufacturers, they would simply cut open the bottle and see which salon the serial number was designated to and revoke their wholesale account.

This is certainly an extreme method of enforcing and protecting the perceived exclusivity and scarcity of a brand but nonetheless powerful and highly valuable. How valuable, you ask? Valuable enough that our mysterious, hulking meeting guests had developed a laser that would erase the serial number without having to open the bottle, allowing my client to sell the stuff completely free of accountability.

Lasers, secret lists, manipulative packaging—some may say this tactic is an example of brands overstepping their bounds. However, some MSVs at other world-renowned luxury brands such as Rolex and Ferrari make their efforts to keep their products off of the secondary market fully known. As part of your sales contract for your new watch or speedy Italian convertible, you are also assigned a serial number as part of a brand registry. Should you resell your asset, it is a demerit on your ability to purchase again, NO EXCEPTIONS! (Just ask Justin Bieber, who is currently banned from buying a Ferrari due to placing his car up for auction months after purchasing it.)

If the method of approachable distinction from Chapter 16 doesn't necessarily scratch your supervillainous itch, perhaps the opposite approach of exclusivity and scarcity will better suit your MSV DNA.

18: PLANET FOUR: PERSONIFICATION

"Well, where did they get the survey cards?"

—"Crazy" Eddie Antar after hearing his customers hated his spokesman so much they said they'd never shop at his stores via in-store survey cards.

Personifying your brand with a real-life spokesperson, animated mascot, or even a live animal (see Bush's Baked Beans and golden retriever Duke) can be a powerful differentiation tactic. It can give a face to your company. Personification can greatly accelerate the emotional connection consumers make with your brand.

This strategy works surprisingly well for brands that sell boring or unapproachable services or products. Most commonly, you can find this strategy used in insurance industries:

- The Geico Gecko
- Flo from Progressive Insurance
- The Aflac Duck
- Liberty Mutual's LiMu Emu

- Jake from State Farm
- J. K. Simmons with Farmers Insurance
- Shaq with The General
- Dennis Haysbert with Allstate
- Allstate's Mayhem character portrayed by Dean Winters (my personal favorite out of all for obvious reasons . . . all hail mayhem!)

Don't be fooled: your choice for personifying your brand doesn't have to be a squeaky-clean spokesman or superhero personality that appeals to all. One of the most successful spokesmen in history rose to become the second most recognized person in the United States, after the acting president (Richard Nixon) at the time. The second most popular person in the country was also the most hated. Universally noted as unbearably irritating, Mr. Whipple from the "Don't Squeeze the Charmin" campaign somehow rocketed the brand to number one. (Sure, they could've used the definitive "the softest," but that differentiator would never have stood the test of time like our dear Mr. Whipple, chastising shoppers for fondling the toilet paper.) The more he invaded people's homes via a 30-second TV spot, the more they hated him . . . but the more they bought.

I'd give the creators of Mr. Whipple an induction into the Marketing Supervillain Hall of Fame, but they too did not understand the correlation. They just shrugged their shoulders and cashed in on the happy accident.[1]

Regardless of which avenue caters to your true authenticity and if you decide to take your persona and make it public-facing, personifying your brand can be a monumental but valuable task that I would encourage you to take on.

MSV Exercise

A mandatory exercise I make all up-and-coming MSVs (aka clients of Decommoditized™) undergo is as follows:

> Without consulting others within the company and assuming you had an unlimited budget, who would the dream spokesperson be for your brand? This candidate can be:
>
> - Alive or dead
> - Real or fictional
> - From any form of media, era, or walk of life

This spokesperson should be a natural extension of your brand and values who can integrate seamlessly with your most devout followers. It should not be someone you would choose solely to capitalize on their existing level of celebrity or influence.

19: PLANET FIVE: LIFESTYLE BRANDING

"The methods of the great pioneers have often puzzled conventional minds."

—Ernst Stavro Blofeld

An underling informs you that they have botched an important task you assigned them. Furious, you raise your gun to his head. Your loyal henchman closes his eyes in silent prayer. You pull the trigger. *BANG!* Your most valued lackey opens his eyes and, in relief, realizes that at the last second, you turned the gun on one of your lowly minions, killing them instead. This is commonly known as the Blofeld Ploy, named after Ernst Stavro Blofeld, an archnemesis of James Bond who utilized this tactic quite often.

The Blofeld Ploy shows that you, the diabolical mastermind, have not gone soft by letting your truly valued allies know how important they are because you are willing to sacrifice another in place of them as a punishment.

Sacrifice will be the theme of this particular method of differentiation: LIFESTYLE.

Turning your brand into a lifestyle is the gold standard when it comes to branding. When creating a lifestyle brand, it may seem logical to make it easily accessible and welcoming to all. This, however, should not be the case.

Much like Mr. Blofeld, you must be willing to sacrifice a large portion of the masses and bet all of your chips on growing a smaller, but higher-valued, pool of prospects for your lifestyle.

In order to create a lifestyle brand with cultlike followers who have an undeniable emotional connection to you or your brand, you must also have a similar group of pagans or nonbelievers who are excluded from your clique. In fact, the more exclusive your lifestyle brand feels, the more your true believers will feel that this culture is more *inclusive*. You create inclusivity by leaning into exclusivity.

Few feel truly passionate about things that are ubiquitous. We've all found an underground band or song that really spoke to us or a small group of folks with our same musical sensibilities.

Then the conundrum of every music fan begins. You value the product of this band so much that you actually will them to succeed. When you play the song for a friend and they too become a fan, somehow you feel like you've won. When the band wins, you feel like you win.

But then, an atrocity occurs. Your band wins a little too big. That special song that was uniquely yours because you discovered it is now the theme song in the latest major car commercial. It's become woven into the pop culture hive mind. It's universally accepted by everyone and is played so much you no longer stop in your tracks when it comes barking out of a radio or television. Hell, you don't even notice it playing at all. It has become uniquely everyone's, which doesn't make it unique at all. It has lost its exclusivity.

The little, exclusive lifestyle tentpole that the band once had (probably because they didn't have the money for marketing) has become one 100% inclusive. The song that made your heart skip a beat in the past hasn't changed, but your passionate loyalty is almost nonexistent. It is no longer unique to you; it has become ubiquitous.

To create a lifestyle brand, your true believers must be more than consumers of your product. They must be personally and emotionally invested in the future success of the brand. In order to accomplish such an emotional bond, you (your brand) must have a set of beliefs or tenets that not only lets followers identify themselves but also identifies the nonbelievers or outsiders with whom we happily do not align and clearly do not welcome with open arms.

To sum up, while it may seem counterintuitive, and likely the last thing you'd read in a marketing manual, exclusion and sacrificing an audience can be incredible marketing tools to help you create a cultlike following. Lucky for you, as a Marketing Supervillain, you do not seek out the conventional methods of the masses or follow the obvious inclinations of what college marketing professors doth profess.

20: PLANET SIX: HERITAGE

*"People of Mars, you say we are brutes and have
a heritage of savagery. But let me tell you one thing:
if I could get loose from this cage you have me in,
I would tear you guys a new Martian asshole."*

—Jack Handey

W hen Barry Becher and Edward Valenti, aka "the Ginsu Guys,"
decided to enter the flatware market in 1978, they knew they
had to differentiate themselves immediately. Table utensils weren't
exactly the most exciting high-priority offerings among the other
television ad products they were competing with on the airwaves.

While they utilized multiple methods of differentiation to
bring their product a miraculous level of success, the duo leaned
into a tactic that made their product infinitely more attractive to the
couch potatoes who were glued to their televisions. Add in a little
mystique and you have a superb recipe for success.

Their method of differentiation? Heritage. Sotheby's has become
the gold standard in the marketplace for buying and selling the
most highly valued pieces of artwork at auction. It is also a premier

example of the use of heritage. Many brands would be content to differentiate themselves with a definitive like "rarest" or "most respected." Sotheby's chose another method of differentiation, the same as our Ginsu Guys: *heritage.*

If you ever take a look at the Sotheby's logo, you will notice a sideways stamp that says "EST: 1744." How much better of a heritage play can you get?

Sotheby's plays in a game of high stakes. Whether you are selling an exquisite piece of artwork or buying a one-of-a-kind sculpture from a Renaissance master, there is an unquestionable element of fear and uncertainty, and the auction house originators wanted to establish the feeling of confidence and safety among their clients. What could be safer than a company that's been around since 1744?

While it may not be immediately obvious, Sotheby's longevity is key to how you perceive them. They exude the characteristics of elevated, respected and, most importantly, experienced. If you're not a seasoned art historian who can appraise a masterpiece, it's not a problem. Remember: Sotheby's is safe because they've been around for over 350 years!

What do you do, however, if you have no real heritage? This is where the genius of our Ginsu Guys shone.

The cutlery startup founded by Barry Becher and Edward Valenti knew that Japanese cutlery had an air of sophistication, dating back to the roots of the fine craftsmanship of samurai swords. The Ginsu Guys knew they wanted some of that for their product.

The problem was (believe it or not!) it was way too cost-prohibitive to manufacture in Japan. Barry and Ed decided to maintain production of their knives in their factory in Arkansas while leaning into an exotic mystique of Japan. They named their product something that sounded as if it were forged by a lineage of expert swordsmen from feudal Japan . . . Ginsu.

The Ginsu corporation was founded and its ads were fast-tracked to your TV sets.

When Barry Becher was asked what Ginsu meant in English, he'd reply, "I never have to work again!" As it turned out, ginsu was a made-up word, not found in Japanese or any other language.[2]

Underhanded? Untruthful? That is a matter of perspective. Successful? The numbers do not lie. Within seven years of their debut in 1978, the Ginsu Guys sold $30 million in knives. Adding heritage as a differentiator, even if it is only implied, can help set a product outside the pack. It worked in spades for the Ginsu Guys.

21: PLANET SEVEN: PROCESS

"I fear not the man who has practiced 10,000 kicks once, but I fear the man who has practiced one kick 10,000 times."

—Bruce Lee

A nother great way to differentiate yourself is by bringing your process to the forefront. If the way you do what you do is special, why not let the masses know? Rolex routinely goes to market for their top-of-the-line products with the slogan *Crafted with scrupulous attention to detail.* Manischewitz markets its kosher products to a traditional audience seeking matzoh and kosher wines with *We make it the old-fashioned way.*

Knowing your audience and what they perceive to be important is pivotal when differentiating with process. One of my favorite instances of differentiation through process comes from the marketing geniuses at the Sweet Amber Distilling Company. When master distiller Dave Pickerell wanted to go to market with a new whiskey, he knew it had to be special and different. Dave knew that hard rock and alcohol went hand in hand, so he approached the megastars of Metallica for a partnership.

The band was interested but didn't want to just slap their name on a label and neither did Dave. Simply having a celeb's name on your product is not a strong method of differentiation. They wanted something revolutionary. After some brainstorming, the group came up with an entirely new method of distilling, a process unlike anything that had been done before. It was a process that required all of their individual DNA and input of each of the two parties.

They came up with the genius idea of bombarding the distilling barrels with ultra-low-frequency sound throughout the distilling process. The sound? Handpicked playlists from the members of Metallica. The goal was to resonate the barrels to extract more of the wood taste into the spirit. They called it Black Noise.

As the stars continued to align for this creative endeavor, one of Metallica's best songs was called "Blackened." Thus, Blackened American Whiskey was born.

Does this process actually work and add to the flavor? I couldn't tell you; my palate is typically refined to Coca-Cola, chicken fingers, and bagel pizzas. Nonetheless, this story is impossible not to share if you happen to bump into someone wearing a Metallica T-shirt at the bar.

22: PLANET EIGHT: NICHING DOWN

"I think getting the audience to chant ECW was really something. I don't care if you draw 70,000 people in a dome for WrestleMania—nobody chants WWE."

—Paul Heyman

Pro wrestling defies logic: two people "fighting" in a ring where the winner has been predetermined, and the "wrestlers" are supposed to present the image of actually trying to hurt each other. Yet, with the World Wrestling Entertainment (or WWE, formerly World Wrestling Federation or WWF) getting close to one billion weekly viewers, professional wrestling is undeniably a revenue-producing powerhouse.

In the 1990s, the professional wrestling industry was in a rut. The over-the-top presentation, heavily influenced by MTV, covered the entire industry like an old, wet carpet. Straightforward, old-school tough guys, like Blackjack Mulligan and Bruno Sanmartino, were replaced by outlandish, cartoonish personas like Irwin R. Schyster (aka I.R.S.) and Isaac Yankem. I.R.S. was the evil, wrestling Internal Revenue Service agent. The product of WWF became a joke and an insult to what had come before it. (Go ahead and guess what Isaac Yankem's schtick was.)

To save this multibillion-dollar industry, something had to change. That change came from a very unlikely place, in the form of one man, Paul Heyman.

So how did one man with practically no resources start a company that challenged WWE as well as Ted Turner's WCW? Not only did he challenge two mega brands, each run by billionaires, he started an industrywide revolution and made a name for himself that is still passionately chanted by rabid fans, 20 years after the brand was acquired.

This is the story of why I will always be a "Paul Heyman Guy."

Paul started as a wrestling photographer and then progressed to manager. He got his big break—or as he put it, the chance to "start a revolution"—when he gained creative control over a very small and severely underfunded regional company in 1993.

Other than the talent who was on his payroll at the time, Paul had very little in the way of resources. His company's show battled for airtime and landed on regional TV at 2:00 a.m. on Saturday nights. Worse, the show aired only in Philadelphia, if it aired at all.

Paul didn't have the glitz, the glam, the pyro, or the money. But he wound up turning the entire industry on its head. His methods and contributions to the sport changed the way things were done, even to this day. Fans worldwide continue to pay tribute to his efforts by passionately screaming the name of his brand, ECW, at shows.

Paul Heyman saw an opportunity. He saw a segment of the audience that was underserved and unheard. Here is the mission statement for his brand:

> "I thought that the business, the industry, the presen-
> tation, needed to change in the same way music had

changed. Music was all about Poison and Mötley Crüe and Winger and all these hair bands, and then along came Nirvana and *BAM!* The whole industry changed. So in the same way, I thought wrestling needed to change, in that wrestling had become the equivalent of hair bands, and we needed wrestling's version of Nirvana to come along and just shake everything up."

As a result, in 1993, the ECW revolution began.

ECW's stripped-down, no-frills, hard-hitting *Fight Club*–style not only covered their glaring weaknesses in production value, but the style actually became an *asset*. To the true fans of the art, it made the WWE and WCW's overdone, goofy personas, outlandish costumes, and correlating storylines look silly. Those fans couldn't have cared less for the expensive fanfare of WWE and WCW.

While Ted Turner, the head of WCW at the time, was studying WWE and trying to one-up their presentation to eke out an extra decimal point in the ratings, Vince McMahon, the head of WWE, was conducting the same study. This copycat style of one-upmanship killed innovation, and Paul wanted no part of it.

Paul led his wrestling revolution and the niche audience of fellow revolters against the cartoonish state of the industry. The true, hardcore fans of wrestling, among which I include myself, would have followed him through the gates of hell.

Why? Because Paul was genuine and aligned with his mission, a key ingredient when you are niching down. When aligning yourself with a leader, whether it be a thought leader in a white-collar business or a leader on the physical front lines willing to take a steel chair to the head, even a slight kink in the armor can become the proverbial fire to your Frankenstein's monster. It could instantly turn your devout followers into a pitchfork-wielding mob, hungry for your severed head.

When Paul got on the mic and pulled back the storyline curtain of the industry, spewing facts about his scripted characters, situations, and politics of every federation, he was believable, and the public respected him for it. He wasn't afraid to air his dirty laundry—as well as his competitors'—for all to see. When you listened to him, you knew what he said was real, or in industry speak, "a total shoot."

Paul, unlike his competition, could not afford highly paid scriptwriters, so everything he did had to be tight. When niching down, everything counts. If the in-ring talent wanted airtime, they had to consistently and, without fail, authentically bring it. And they did.

This unusual level of reality in a world built on total fantasy shone through the product and the audiences took to it immediately. The unheard, unserved niches had found their visionary. Crowd sizes grew in leaps and bounds. Soon the big guys with all of the resources were looking to Paul's product, copying ideas, and poaching his talent.

Today, Paul continues to be successful and influential in the industry. He is looked upon as a revolutionary and a genius. Many people still carry the torch of his brand ECW, thousands proudly wearing "I'm A Paul Heyman Guy" T-shirts. It's both a tribute to the man as well as a statement that lets others know that they too are a little different, they are authentic, and they see things through a unique lens.

It's with pride that I admit, on those tough days where it actually does seem like I am truly alone in the way I see things, I proudly put on my "I'm A Paul Heyman Guy" T-shirt and continue forward. Paul has demonstrated, with amazing results, that niching down and focusing on what counts—even in the face of ridicule—is the way to true differentiation.

23: PLANET NINE: REPOSITIONING THE CATEGORY

"I don't want to be a product of my environment. I want my environment to be a product of me."

—Jack Nicholson as Frank Costello in The Departed

In marketing, the word "repositioning" gets thrown around a lot. It usually refers to a situation when a dying brand decides to change up its game. The main goal is to change either how the consumers perceive the brand or what the brand is actually offering to its customers.

Let's take Spotify as an example. With the changing habits of its users during the COVID pandemic, the popular music streaming app noticed a dramatic drop in ad revenue. Where Spotify previously rested on offering the industry's best streaming music selection and experience to its users, the company now decided to emulate Netflix's business model and reposition itself as an original content provider.

Spotify capitalized on this buzz with a coinciding repositioning campaign to help pivot the company's focus and change what consumers thought of the platform, leading to an almost immediate increase in revenue. This strategy paid off, and Spotify saw its ad revenue rise 9 percent to $185 million in Q3 from the previous year.

Spotify is an example of repositioning a brand, but what happens when you need to reposition an entire category?

In 1964, the toy company Hasbro had a problem on its hands. They had purchased the rights to a property that began as a comic strip honoring the men and women serving in the U.S. military.

Their plan was to create miniaturized figures of army, navy, air force, and marine soldiers so children could create their own imaginary backyard battlefields. At that time, however, it wasn't exactly common, cool, or socially acceptable for young boys—the intended audience—to be playing with dolls.

At the time, any miniaturized version of a human form was referred to as a doll. There simply was no other word for it. Boys had been conditioned to see these dolls as "girl toys" and as such, parents were not motivated to purchase dolls for their sons.

Enter Hasbro's CEO, Don Levine. Since he had already paid for the license, he tasked his marketing department with the feat of coming up with a solution to this $100,000 identity crisis. They came back with a method of differentiation I call "Repositioning the Category."

Rather than fight an uphill battle to change the population's perception of "dolls," Hasbro coined a new term, "action figure," and used it to introduce young boys across the globe to G.I. Joe, A Real American Hero.

Today, children and toy collectors, myself included, can thank Hasbro for not only creating G.I. Joe but for spawning an entirely new doll category, known the world over as "action figures."

I've always been more of a Cobra Commander type of guy. Regardless, now you know, and knowing is half the battle.

24: PLANET TEN: TIMING

> *"I never wanted to be the next Bruce Lee.
> I just wanted to be the first Jackie Chan."*
>
> **—Jackie Chan**

Timing as a differentiator is something we've all experienced as consumers. At one time or another, a brand has attempted to stand out in its respective vertical by saying they were the originator of the product or service in question. Philadelphia Cream Cheese makes sure you know they invented the creamy white stuff on every package. What they don't tell you is that they actually invented it in New York. And just like the Ginsu Guys in Chapter 20, they decided to manufacture additional heritage and adopted the Philadelphia brand because the city was more synonymous with quality food at that time. (Yes, even cream cheese has villainous roots!)

Some additional forms of timing as a differentiator can be:

- The First
- The Latest
- The Originators

- The Inventors
- The Oldest
- The Newest
- What's Next
- The Future

The use of timing can be a very simple way to establish trust and credibility with your demographic. However as with any powerful weapon, it cuts both ways.

Let's take a look at Harley-Davidson, a brand entrenched in tradition and timing. Harley-Davidson is credited as the originator of the ubiquitous chopper style of customized motorcycle. For multiple generations, it has been the gold standard and the American staple of motorbikes.

This incredible achievement has served the brand in stellar fashion for over a century. However, the very differentiator that contributed to their success has become an albatross around their neck. The problem? The generation gap.

As of 2022, Harley-Davidson experienced their 14th consecutive year of declining sales. As their tried-and-true loyalists and enthusiasts began to age out, millennials and Gen Z have entered the marketplace.

Culture and values shift with generations. The newer, younger demographic did not place much of an emphasis on tradition. The brand of counterculture thinking on which Harley so proudly built its 120-year reputation had now become *the culture*. The new generation wanted a different counterculture. In short, post-baby boomers did not want to drive the same bikes their fathers and grandfathers drove. They wanted something different. The HOGs (Harley Owners Groups) who came before them drove these gas-guzzling, non-eco-friendly machines without a care in the world. However, millennials and Gen Zers no longer align with this value.

Harley-Davidson knew it had a massive problem on its hands. How did they appeal to the new generation's values without alienating their previous demographic? Electric bikes for eco-conscious millennials flopped. Mobile apps, classes, clubs and communities were given a makeover in an ongoing quest to find the delicate balance of messaging that appealed to the passionate, hard-core believers as well as the curious newcomers. It's an issue that, at the time of this writing, has not been successfully navigated. (Perhaps they should consider hiring this MSV to help them!)

As MSVs, we can learn a valuable lesson from this. Timing as a differentiator can be a powerful and profitable weapon. When choosing to use this tactic, however, you should also use its power to forecast the positioning. Do everything possible to ensure that what resonates today will not alienate tomorrow's generations. You can use timing in your differentiation process to help bring your brand into uncharted waters where no other competitor can venture. Like any great boat captain (or MSV), always be sure to chart the waters ahead. The same tide that led you to treasure may also lead you to peril.

25: PLANET ELEVEN: CAUSE ALIGNMENT

"Everyone has a purpose in life. Perhaps yours is watching television."

—David Letterman

Dawn Soap is synonymous with images of cute ducklings getting cleaned of environmental pollutants. It's marketed not only as the purest blend of ingredients but also safe enough for a sensitive baby animal's skin. Dawn organically fell into the body of water of *cause alignment* after wildlife experts proclaimed their soap to be the best for the job.

Take a stroll into the frozen foods aisle, and you'll no doubt come across another example of differentiation through cause alignment. Ben & Jerry's Ice Cream is a shining example of corporate social responsibility. Ben & Jerry's has aligned itself with multiple causes, from global peace to same-sex marriages and non-GMO foods. Cause alignment has become ingrained in their brand.

Aligning your brand with a cause is easy. It's the lowest-hanging fruit of differentiation and quite en vogue at the moment. It's understandable: cause alignment can appear easy and even righteous. After all, how could helping others cause harm? But when used incorrectly, cause alignment can be perceived as inauthentic and manipulative.

In 2022, Unilever made a push for all 400 of its brands to each have a socially or environmentally aligned cause. Investors were not particularly moved or impressed, and the *Wall Street Journal* addressed the topic with an article titled "Does Your Mayonnaise Really Need a Mission Statement?"

Cause alignment is reaching its tipping point. Remember that when everyone is differentiating themselves the same way, then no one is truly differentiated.

Any brand can attach itself to a cause and do something philanthropic. But in this instance, we're talking about aligning with a cause so strongly that it becomes part of your ongoing marketing and brand DNA. Executed correctly, cause alignment can create cultlike followers for your brand.

My favorite example of how you can decommoditize the overuse of cause alignment as a differentiator also happens to be one of my personal heroes. He converted me into a fist-pumping, cultlike follower for his unconventional cause and associated brand.

Lloyd Kaufman is a pioneer in underground cinema. By using slime, fake blood, toxic waste, and Bromo-Seltzer (and cause alignment), he made his way to cult icon status in his vertical.

Lloyd Kaufman (affectionately referred to as Uncle Lloyd by his legions of niche audience devotees) is the creator of *The Toxic Avenger* and founder of Troma Studios. Lloyd Kaufman is the epitome of a differentiator. Where Warner Brothers had the clean-cut, perfectly groomed, and mild-mannered Clark Kent, aka Superman, Uncle Lloyd introduced us to a very unlikely superhero, The Toxic Avenger, a nerd who had been dipped into toxic waste and transformed into a monster who beat his victims with a dirty mop and their own limbs after he had ripped them from their bodies.

Unconventional and outlandish are not the typical descriptors you would use for great social cause leaders. For the past forty years, Lloyd has taken every chance to flip a giant middle finger to the formulaic, predictable tastes of the Hollywood studio film production system as well as the sensibilities of mainstream audiences.

What was Troma and Lloyd's completely authentic cause alignment? It was the fight for the true independence of smaller, more offbeat filmmakers. He is driven by an uncompromising desire to level the playing field and help filmmakers who are Hollywood outsiders get seen by a much larger audience. Even if you were a filmmaker or cinephile who did not enjoy the taste of Troma's products, which is undoubtedly acquired (just ask my editor), you couldn't help but align yourself with their cause.

Lloyd's authentic passion and cause alignment were contagious. They attracted and inspired others with similar mindsets, not just as customers but also as employees. In 1996, Troma welcomed James Gunn, a young filmmaker-to-be who aligned with everything Troma stood for. They gave him the chance to write and create *Tromeo and Juliet* under Lloyd's direction.

By 2023, Lloyd's protégé became the most sought-after director in Hollywood. Gunn found tremendous success as a writer and director by using the skills he gained from working with Lloyd at Troma.

Lloyd's continued commitment to the cause is steadfast. Lloyd is an uncommon man whose cause alignment rings true with a unique audience. In an offering as uncommon as the man himself, Lloyd continues to help bolster the projects of creators outside the Hollywood system with a standing offer to appear in any independent filmmaker's creation, completely free of charge (sans travel expenses).

Lloyd's cause alignment of propping up the "little guy" has paved the way for little-known filmmakers to become brand names. He is a prime example of authentic cause alignment as an effective method of differentiation.

26: PLANET TWELVE: BYPRODUCT

"Immortality is the byproduct of doing good work."
—Mel Brooks

I saved the most important—and the most difficult—differentiator for last. While the Universe of Differentiation is a free-form guide to help a brand choose a differentiator, I require all of my clients to visit the planet we are about to discuss. I provide the same guidance to you.

A byproduct is *an incidental or secondary product created in the manufacture or synthesis of something else.*

All products, services and brands create byproducts. These are the subliminal features or benefits that motivate or inspire a potential prospect to choose your brand over someone else's. Think of byproducts as the benefits your product or service offers that wouldn't be put into an ad.

Here is a recent example:

I was working within the commoditized industry of law firms. The client firm knew that they were completely undifferentiated, as most law firms are. Watch any commercial for a law firm; you can mute the volume and still predict what they are saying.

This particular firm was already experiencing the pain of commoditization and had started to think in a better direction. They wanted to narrow their service offerings solely to general contractors and builders. It was a great starting point for us to proceed through our process of differentiation.

For me, however, providing legal services to GCs and builders was not their real product. Their real *marketable* differentiated product was actually a *byproduct* of this service. In a guided meeting, I coached them through the process of discovering their byproducts. In most cases, the first round of answers is rarely close to the bull's-eye, so be sure to hold your client or (if you are attempting to do this for your non-agency business) yourself accountable during this exercise! Here are some of the round-one mistakes:

- Access: We answer the phone! (INCORRECT)
- Boutique Service: no paralegals, you work directly with an attorney. (INCORRECT)
- We Fight Hard: We're no pushovers, we fight harder! (VERY INCORRECT)
- Experience: We've done this so long, we're clearly better. (INCORRECT)

While the above statements may be completely fine for ad copy, any of the firm's competitors could use these statements, which would not differentiate the firm. Worse, none of the statements answered the most important question: **When a client chooses me, what anxieties am I reducing for them?** After some deep soul-searching, we began to uncover the gold. (By the way, if the search for your byproduct was easy and quick, there's a strong chance that you really haven't found it. Dig deeper.)

We realized that most contractors who hire general counsel were all the same age. They were all experiencing "the seven-year itch." This was a great discovery, as it niched down our audience even further. Now we just needed to figure out why this pattern existed.

We learned that after seven years in business, this industry ran into a particular and specific set of challenges usually related to scaling. Although these companies were growing, they did not yet have the financial resources to engage a law firm as an integral part of their team. These particular contractors had the foundation (pun intended) but were stuck. Traditionally, this size of contractor hired a law firm only when they had a need. ("I'm being sued!"). The common relationship was a reactive one.

The product this particular law firm was offering was a cost-effective manner to have legal counsel as an integrated part of the GC's team. What we discovered, however, was that the *byproduct* of this service was assuring the growing GC that they now had the authority to pursue higher levels of excellence.

How did this newfound piece of branding gold help our law firm? When the firm pitched their presentation, two things happened. First, they pitched only at conferences that contained their target vertical audience: construction firms in the adolescent stage of their growth cycle, who had X dollars of revenue and X number of employees. Second, the firm immediately differentiated itself by changing the focus of the conversation to the *byproduct*: a qualified legal team that provided GCs the confidence to go after larger and larger jobs, knowing that their legal "back" was always covered.

In our personification exercise, we uncovered their fictional spokesperson to be Alfred Pennyworth (Batman's butler), and all of our messaging was molded to sound authentic, as if it were coming directly from Alfred's mouth. The law firm's presence and the comfort and confidence of someone like Alfred taking care of the back office empowered the GC to become all they could be. The typical gloom and doom pitches from other niche firms forecasting inevitable lawsuits paled in comparison to our firm's message of potential growth and support.

27: DECOMMODITIZED METHODS OF MARKETING MISCHIEF #1: IRRITATING AN AUDIENCE FOR FUN AND PROFIT

"I've never been in a band that's been in tune."
—Peter Steele

The importance of knowing how to please audiences cannot be overstated. Much like creating great music, however, business and marketing is not only about knowing which keys create consonance but also being keenly aware of which ones create dissonance.

Take fast-food giant Wendy's.

The Marketing Supervillains in charge of Wendy's Twitter account know that irritating an audience is a great way to differentiate yourself in a crowded, noisy space. Most consumers ingest the corporate mumbo-jumbo of commoditized, predictable content with the same expectation: to be gently, but assuredly, lulled to sleep. It's great reading when your sleeping pills have quit doing their job.

Knowing how to spike your customer's attention is paramount to MSV success … even if it entails irritating or downright infuriating your audience.

"How much does a Big Mac cost?" asked one user inquiring about a competitor's popular product.

Wendy's ingeniously replied: "Your dignity."

It's a tweet that went out years ago along with an abundance of other snarky remarks. I liked this one so much that, to this day, I still bring it up at parties. In contrast, McDonald's, at the time of this writing, is closing in on one million tweets and I cannot remember a single damn one. But I can fall fast asleep reading their corporate mumbo-jumbo.

While I don't ingest fast food as part of my daily diet, what I do "ingest," in large quantities, is music. One of my favorite auditory meals is the music of Type O Negative, a band that exquisitely demonstrates how to aggravate your fan base for fun and, most importantly, profit.

When I was 18, MTV's *Headbangers Ball* was my go-to source for music. Yet, whenever a certain band came on, I headed to the fridge for a snack. This particular sound stopped my caffeine-fueled Saturday night headbanging by taking the tempo down a notch … or ten. The band in question was often referred to as the Drab Four, an indication that they were intentionally being the polar opposite of the Beatles' notable, cheery upbeat tempos.

Type O Negative's first CD described their style: *Slow, Deep, and Hard*. While I initially hated their sound, I gained great respect for their marketing genius and am now and will forever be a true believer.

Type O Negative released a live album. But instead of releasing the typical blockbuster live show with fans screaming their affection, the band deliberately played in front of a crowd that was chosen because they were in no way interested in Type O Negative. In reality, this recording was painstakingly re-created in a studio environment and based on the real hostility the band experienced on their European tour. It was so raw and well done it might as well have been 100% genuine. While the production was not authentic, the consistency in the band's messaging was.

The lead singer, Peter Steele, took tremendous joy in irritating the rabid crowd. He'd throw fuel on the fire of angry fans by deliberately performing slow, tedious renditions of "I'm in the Mood for Love."

My personal favorite part of that show was when an audience member could clearly be heard calling Pete an asshole. Pete stopped the show and pointed out to that "fan" that he paid $15 to get inside, while Type O Negative was *getting paid* to be there. Pete proudly asked, "Who's the real asshole in this scenario?"

What better way to entertain an audience of counterculture music devotees than ruthlessly forcing it down the throats of the mainstream audience both you and your fans are rebelling against and enjoying the fallout together?

As you approach the world of marketing with your new supervillain lens, you will begin to see marketing antagonists everywhere making huge strides and attracting loyal believers. From fast-food MSVs like Wendy's to technology giants like Apple with its Mac versus PC campaign, MSVs lurk everywhere. Playfully chastising the tastes of a competitor's audience, while expertly creating dissonance within a demographic, is always a surefire method of differentiation.

28: DECOMMODITIZED METHODS OF MARKETING MISCHIEF #2: BREAKING BROCA

"I must break you."
—Ivan Drago, Rocky IV

In Chapter 6, I spoke about how I achieved success with a quirky tactic to differentiate my piece of mail from all others. The fact that the letter was to Weird Al certainly doesn't help my case as to why differentiation is *not* about being the standout weirdo in the bunch.

For now, let's accept the premise that standing out from the crowd can be created through weirdness. But more importantly, let's examine on a more primal level what happens when you differentiate yourself through outlandishness.

Broca's area (which I'll call Broca for short) is an important part of the brain that everyone facing commoditization or seeking market differentiation should know about.

One of the main functions of Broca is to anticipate and discount the predictable. Without it, you would surely go mad (and not the good MSV mad that comes with power and a great maniacal laugh!). Without Broca's area, the brain wouldn't filter any stimuli. Instead, it would process every single thing coming at you—just like in the caveman days when every element in the environment could potentially kill you.

Today, the average person sees 10,000 ads per day. Broca's area works overtime to weed out the white noise and keep you from going insane due to overload. For example, can you remember more than five of the 10,000 ads you were exposed to yesterday? If not, thank Broca.

In some ways, the brain, like a muscle, would prefer to be lazy. Even though you may make your abdominal muscles do crunches, they don't actually *want* to do that work. When they get overworked, they send you pain signals, trying to get you to stop. Similarly, your brain doesn't actually want to work hard and pay attention to every little message or stimulus it receives. That's why, when it is overstimulated, it will often send you the pain signal of a headache, in an effort to get you to stop.

When Broca begins to hear or see things it thinks it's seen before, it predicts what's coming and attempts to push the fast-forward button and move onto something else, seeking something truly worthy of its attention. Basically, its job is to act as a filter to prevent overload, like the circuit breaker on your electrical box.

One of the most successful examples of Breaking Broca comes from the '80s. If, at the time, you watched network television, you couldn't avoid commercials for the Ginsu Knife. The secret to the commercial's success was the opening seconds where a voice-over proclaimed, "In Japan, the hand can be used like a knife." A tomato sitting on a cutting board was karate chopped by someone's hand, creating a mess.

These opening seconds succeeded in Breaking Broca. It caused the viewer, who was most likely in Beta mode (the mode the brain enters when it feels it does not need to be truly engaged) to snap into a new brain frequency and pay attention (aka: Alpha mode).

Humans at large spend nearly half of their lives in Beta mode. In his book, *Your Brain at Work*, David Rock found that a whopping 46.9% of daily life is governed by Broca, which keeps us all in autopilot mode. The "Ginsu Guys" were able to crack the code and "Break Broca" out of Beta and into Alpha. They literally "broke the brain wave pattern" to get your attention. Thirty million dollars in sales later, the Ginsu Corporation was sold to Warren Buffet's Berkshire Hathaway in 1985.

For MSVs, understanding how to break Broca provides a massive opportunity to interrupt and capitalize on this zombie-like state of the populace, get their attention with our differentiated messaging and race past Broca and go directly to the bank.

*Editor's note: There is ongoing debate of the prime roles of Broca in the brain, whether it is relegated to only language processing or if it is also involved in action observation and planning.

**Author's note: My editor mysteriously disappeared last night after trying to correct me. Disregard the note above.

29: DECOMMODITIZED METHODS OF MARKETING MISCHIEF #3: THE TROJAN HORSE

"I prefer a real villain to a false hero."
—Killer Mike

T he Trojan horse doesn't conjure thoughts of honorable warfare. It's definitely not something you'd associate with one of the top 100 most loved brands in the world. But at age 11, I was fully caught in the crosshairs of a diabolical marketing scheme that took the public by storm.

The year: 1985.

The place: Japan. Nintendo had built a superior gaming system that the Japanese public loved.

THE NEXT STEP? CONQUER THE U.S. MARKET

The United States home video game market had become a bloated, commoditized marketplace. Nintendo was so desperate for entry that it approached the retail toy giant FAO Schwarz and offered to stock its shelves with their merchandise for free, with the singular goal of simply getting a piece of FAO Schwarz's shelf space. That should've sounded like an all-profit play for the giant toy retailer. Can you guess how FAO Schwarz responded? They declined!

Nintendo knew they had a HUGE problem. How could they differentiate themselves in a saturated market? They were sure that if people just gave their hardware a shot, they'd be hooked.

ENTER THE TROJAN HORSE

Nintendo's solution was to give the public something they'd never seen before: a robot that actually plays video games with you. He was called ROB, the Robotic Operating Buddy.

ROB got people to stop and take notice. It seemed every newscast was asking, "Who wouldn't want a robotic video game pal?"

The buzz was so incredible and unstoppable that the Christmas after launching ROB (yes, through FAO Schwarz), an FAO Schwarz representative was quoted as saying they had never worked so hard before or since. Even little Jesse James Wroblewski plunked down his dollars for a system.

So far, nothing too noteworthy or villainous. Here's the rub:

With 800 officially licensed games on the Nintendo Entertainment System (NES), how many of them do you think you could actually play with ROB? One hundred? Two hundred? Three hundred?

Two. Just two.

And to make matters worse, you'd be hard-pressed to find any video gamer who will admit that either of those two games was remotely enjoyable to play.

Nintendo had pulled the wool over everyone's eyes, including mine. Their Trojan horse, ROB, got me to let down my guard and open my piggy bank. ROB quickly started collecting dust at the bottom of my closet as I became obsessed with Nintendo's other amazing games. The diabolical plan was executed just as they intended. They had infiltrated my bank account and now I was hooked.

FLASH FORWARD TO TODAY

Was Nintendo's Trojan horse a level of DIABOLICAL DIFFERENTIATION? Possibly. Did it work? Absolutely. Nintendo went from the brink of extinction to a mainstay in the top 100 most valuable and most loved brands in the world.

THE TAKEAWAY

It doesn't matter if you're an 11-year-old video gamer or a seasoned professional. We've all been conditioned to raise our defenses when approached by a new sales tactic. Nintendo knew this and brilliantly overcame this obstacle, which led to market domination in a commoditized marketplace. Sure, you might not exactly have a giant Trojan horse or a robot, but you *do* have your own version of these. Today's ethical Trojan horses come in the form of thought leadership pieces, white papers, or published books. It is these offerings that move your brand to break through the guarded defenses of your audience. Once inside, you can then create the opportunity to demonstrate your true creative power.

30: DECOMMODITIZED METHODS OF MARKETING MISCHIEF #4: MYSTERY

"[People] automatically assume that a magician keeps secrets from people. But a real magician keeps secrets for people."

—Derek DelGaudio

Stonehenge. The lost city of Atlantis. The identity of Jack the Ripper. And my personal favorite mystery, what's in the box at the end of the movie *Se7en*?

In my supervillain lair, a plain cardboard box with a giant question mark emblazoned upon it stands proudly on one of my shelves. While most would immediately think it's some sort of murder memorabilia left behind at a crime scene by the Riddler, it is not.

It is a mystery box from NYC's oldest magic shop, Tannen's. It's a brilliant marketing tactic Tannen's uses to give the buyer $50 worth of magic tricks for just $25. The hook, however, is you don't know what you're getting. But in my opinion, the most noteworthy detail about the box is how the creator of *Lost*, JJ Abrams, made it famous in his TED talk.

JJ notes how the mystery box shaped his writing style—mainly, how the wonderment and stickiness of a good mystery is the most important part of any story.

The world of marketing is no stranger to mystery. For example:

- Coca-Cola publicizes how they lock their "Secret Formula" away in a massive bank vault in Atlanta. They even turned it into a theme park–like attraction where you can attempt to break in and steal the prized recipe.
- KFC will never surrender the Colonel's secret blend of 11 herbs and spices.
- And the secret sauce will always be a special and intriguing part of a McDonald's Big Mac.

Do these mysteries contribute to profits? I don't know for sure, but what I *do* know is that Coke is ahead of Pepsi, KFC is ahead of Boston Market, and McDonald's is ahead of Burger King. So anecdotally, I would have to say yes.

Most people ask if I have opened my Tannen's mystery box. Nope, and I probably never will, because it serves as a reminder that mystery is indeed more important than the knowledge of what's inside. By the way, I can tell you by the weight that it's definitely not Gwyneth Paltrow's head.

31: DECOMMODITIZED METHODS OF MARKETING MISCHIEF #5: OVERPROMISING

"If you experience an erection lasting more than four hours, please consult a physician."

—Pfizer

As you now know, I have a penchant for cinema. Add a villain into the mix and you've got my ticket money. My favorite genre is horror because all the best villains reside there.

As I was dusting off the pristine collection of horror props and mementos in my supervillain lair, I came across a relic from the bygone drive-in days: a genuine promotional vomit bag. This item was handed out free with any ticket purchased for Herschell Gordon Lewis's 1963 masterpiece, *Blood Feast*.

Aside from the freebie being a genius and cost-effective way to build buzz around the low-budget splatter fest, it set the tone for a much deeper method of marketing mischief that is responsible for helping one product amass close to $2 billion in revenue.

The free vomit bag, handed out with your ticket purchase, implanted the notion that this movie was going to be so violent and gory, it would surpass anything you had seen before. It placed audiences in a completely different mindset. While traditional moviegoers, parting with their money and free time, would wonder if a movie was going to deliver at all, the daring vomit bag holders of *Blood Feast* knew the movie was absolutely going to deliver. The only question they were left to ponder was, could they withstand the onslaught of gore? Would it truly turn their stomach as the imprint on the bag implied? Would it ruin their evening? Or would they survive and live to joke about it to their friends later?

This is a prime example of overpromising, a bona fide method of marketing mischief.

Flash forward 40 years to 2003. When the marketers at Pfizer came up with their "almost too good to be true" miracle cure for erectile dysfunction, Viagra, they knew they would also be met with some skepticism. Taking a page from the Grandfather of Gore's book, they decided to put a warning in all of the ads:

"If you experience an erection lasting more than four hours, please consult a physician."

Most men quickly went from "Does this stuff work?" to "This could give me an erection for four hours!" The question of whether it worked quickly became a foregone conclusion. The thinking shifted to "I wonder how well it could work for me?" This subliminally implanted question quickly helped the little blue pill reach total revenues of close to $2 billion.

While the *Blood Feast* barf bag passively planted the seed in viewers that the movie in question was so brutal it would ruin their evening, Pfizer's iconic extreme case study challenged customers that it could enhance their night so much that a trained medical professional might be required.

Two diametrically opposed angles, utilizing the same overpromising tactic for monumental results. While *Blood Feast* soaked drive-in screens with gore starting in 1963, the recorded incidents of moviegoers actually utilizing the souvenir sick bags due to the extreme content have migrated from factual statistic to cinematic folklore over the years. The movie continues to screen at midnight movie theaters across the country.

Similarly, due to the HIPAA, we can't know for sure how many people have called their general practitioners in a panic after over four hours of bedroom fun. But we do know that Pfizer amassed a multibillion-dollar fortune off the back of their little blue pill, thanks to overpromising.

32: THE MSV HALL OF SHAME

*"Nothing says 'you're a loser' more than owning
a motivational poster about being a winner."*
—Justin Sewell

Accepting the lifestyle of an MSV can become intoxicating. But before you get all excited about your new mindset and your personal arsenal of decommoditizing weaponry and run off into the battle we call marketing, remember this: A thousand-mile journey starts with a single step, but so does falling in a ditch and breaking your neck.

Allow me to guide you through the most common pitfalls and ditches to help you avoid breaking that neck of yours on your first steps.

Below are some regrettable MSV personas who leapt for the easy, low-hanging fruit of decommoditization. Their corpses are currently littering the base of the ditch, so let's learn from their rookie mistakes.

REGRETTABLE MSV PERSONA #1:
THE MAGICIAN

I love magicians. These performers get up onstage and let you know straightaway that they are going to deceive you. Then they do exactly that, and you are happier for it.

As I delved deeper into adding some of these crowd-pleasing yet underhanded feats to my marketing repertoire, I discovered why an escape artist gives you 100 feet of rope when they ask you to tie them up. You see, the longer the rope, the more difficult it is to keep taut, and the easier the escape.

What do magicians and rope have to do with differentiation and business?

Stay with me. There is a key point here.

The year was 1991. Philips released a monstrous piece of technology onto the market called the CD-i. When it came to market differentiation, the CD-i had it all: Heritage, Process, The Latest and Greatest, and Timing.

It was so powerful that Philips marketed the device as "The Imagination Machine." According to Philips, it could do *anything within the limits of your own imagination.*

And therein was the problem. The "limits of your own imagination" seemed rather limitless. In fact, it felt daunting. By asking their customers to figure out what to do with CD-i, Philips unwittingly gave their audience too much responsibility—too much rope. You can guess what happened next.

While Philips caught their audience's attention, they also failed miserably because they left it to their customers' imaginations of what to do with so much power. When you leave something to the creativity of your customer, they will either screw it up or do nothing. Philips's customers did both and slipped out of the company's grasp. Ah, the paradox of choice.

The iPhone, which debuted in 2009, was also a feature-rich product that had it all. Unlike Philips, however, Apple resisted the urge to tout everything the device could do. They simply approached the market with this slogan:

"There's an app for that."

The campaign let potential customers know that for any issue they came across in their daily life, the iPhone had the answer.

Need to calculate a tip? Split a check? Calculate tolls on a long road trip? Know the best point in a movie to run and use the bathroom?

"There's an app for that."

In the process of differentiation, you have to keep your clients focused. Resist the urge to tout every single thing you have going for you. Shorten that rope. Avoid the tendencies of "The Magician" or just like the CD-i, *poof!* Your business could disappear from the market.

REGRETTABLE MSV PERSONA #2:
THE ECONOMIST

The most common question about the Universe of Differentiation is "Why is there no planet for pricing? Can pricing be a differentiator?"

Yes, but pricing is a terrible motivator—so much that, like the planet Pluto, it has been ousted from planetary status.

"The Economist" persona is quick to ask, "But what about Walmart? Walmart is an incredibly valued brand with the bank account to back it up."

Walmart is a household name and ubiquitous with our culture. What, however, do you think would happen if a supervillain such as myself were to create J-Mart and offer even lower prices than Walmart? How many of the "loyal" Walmart shoppers would continue to patronize the store they all know and love? How many, without even checking into my diabolical background, would simply switch to J-Mart overnight without a second thought simply because they can get frozen pizzas for $1 cheaper than the alternative?

The goal of being a differentiating MSV is to make the customer permanent to your brand; to make competing with you simply not possible. What is more possible than lowering your price? What is easier to compete with than a race to the bottom for the cheapest solution? So uncreative, so un-MSV-esque.

Yes, pricing can be a differentiator, but if you are looking to build a brand with any type of loyalty, consider another planet in the Universe of Differentiation and avoid thinking like "The Economist."

REGRETTABLE MSV PERSONA #3:
THE ASSOCIATE OF J.D. POWER

Unless it's an Academy Award or an Emmy, keep your awards to yourself. It's so easy to run a film festival or awards ceremony that laurels and trophies have become commoditized. "Award-winning agency" no longer has the clout it once did. Having your film as an official selection at a random film fest carries about as much weight as a J.D. Power and Associates award. Lest you forget, we are in a society where everyone wins an award, even if it's just for participation.

I actually came across a porn star's Twitter account whose bio read, "Award-Winning Adult Film Star." As if someone looking at her in their most primal state would think, "Well, she's really not my type but she *did* win an award . . . Maybe I should reconsider?"

REGRETTABLE MSV PERSONA #4:
THE CAMP COUNSELOR

Culture is important. But not to your consumer. The Camp Counselor persona tends to ignore the latter. There are countless online articles about how corporate culture can absolutely be a competitive differentiator. Post-COVID, the number of those articles has exploded as workforces have been functioning from their homes. Culture seems to be in jeopardy, and everyone is in a panic.

Culture is how things get done when no one is looking. A happier team creating the products can indeed lead to better-made products. This differentiating factor is for you, the CEO, your managers, and the rest of your team. As a consumer, how much of a premium are you willing to pay for the *culture* of the manufacturers of your products?

It is common knowledge that Chinese factory workers are absolutely miserable creating smartphones. Some well-documented cases of workers leaping to their deaths have not impacted iPhone sales in the least. Would you consider paying more for a phone made by happier employees? What if it wasn't as advanced as the ones made by the sadder team? If you said no, it's not just the supervillain in you. It's the true value of culture as a differentiator to consumers.

Ask yourself: Do you really care if your cell phone plan with AT&T is supported by technicians who are happier than the ones working at Verizon or T-Mobile? If "Team Sad Sacks" offered better reception at the same price, how long would you consider before making the move?

Sure, you may pay more attention or even a slight premium in price to a brand whose culture aligns with charitable acts that in turn align with your values (cause alignment), but for how long? What will you do once a slightly better, more cost-efficient, or more convenient option comes along? Culture is great. A great culture can create greater things. And those things can create great relationships with customers. But your clients don't care that you sing campfire songs on Fridays with your team. They only care about the product or service they receive. Culture can be the wizard behind the curtain but not the performer at the front of the stage. Culture can indeed be a major differentiator in recruiting others to join your team. However, it should not be the center of your consumer-facing differentiation strategy.

REGRETTABLE MSV PERSONA #5: MR. MORE-BETTER

"We're More Better Than Them!"

Epic last words chiseled into the tombstone of this fallen MSV persona, Mr. More-Better.[3]

Possibly the biggest mistake in the Universe of Differentiation— the entire universe, really—is proclaiming you are "more better" than the other options in the market when it comes to differentiating yourself.

Imagine the big proposal is down to you and a competitor. The decision maker is on the fence about who to choose. You roll your eyes because *clearly* they should choose you. Even though you offer the same service as your competitor, your final results are always more better than your competitor's.

The problem is your competitor is saying the same exact thing. What if they are claiming they are **more better** in a way that's **more better** than you can explain?

Look elsewhere for a differentiator, for here lies Mr. More-Better. Rest in peace.

(Credit to David C. Baker for this intentionally grammatically incorrect but brilliant naming convention.)

REGRETTABLE MSV PERSONA #6: THE GREATEST DIFFERENTIATOR ON YOUR ENTIRE BLOCK

A common pitfall when using definitives as differentiation is a deep-rooted fear that someone will challenge your definitive claim and expose you publicly as a liar. It's a completely understandable fear. It's also never realized.

Even so, left unchecked, this fear ultimately spelled doom for "The Greatest Differentiator on Your Entire Block." Here is how to avoid his horrible fate:

Choosing a successful, differentiated definitive for yourself or your brand should, *deep down*, scare you. If it doesn't, it's not ambitious enough. You're thinking too small. Your definitive should be scary enough to keep you on your toes and motivate you to actually become that definitive. This fear will cause you to strategize your sentiments before opening your mouth or publishing your next LinkedIn post. Eventually, you'll rise to embody your chosen title and realize you were indeed thinking too small in the first place.

For close to 50 years, KISS has been known as "The World's Most Dangerous Band." Why? Simply because they said they were and the press ran with it and, as the saying goes, the rest is history. Radio "Shock Jock" Howard Stern is known as "The King of All Media" but not because he was elected as such from a selection of competitors. He decided that was how he wanted to be known, and he simply crowned himself with the grandiose title.

When it comes to describing themselves, MSVs are rarely subtle, nor should they be! MSV Hall of Famer and master pitchman Ron Popeil titled his autobiography *The Salesman of the Century*.

Currently, I am working to rebrand a large tech firm that is now coming into their own within their vertical. The unique way they have offered service to their client base over the years has now become an industry standard. Their experience and expertise truly grant them the permission to embody the definitive I (and the overwhelming evidence) chose for them:

"The Global Leaders in Dynamic Data Activation"

The stakeholders pushed back, wanting to downsize the claim to "The *National* Leaders in Dynamic Data Activation." It was as if they felt there was a legion of actual global leaders in this vertical who would discuss my client's claim at their next clandestine meeting before casting them out of the club. At the same time, they also envisioned that a smaller, less decorated, national branch wouldn't raise an eyebrow at their claim. This simply is not going to happen, so think BIG and SCARY!

I've attended concerts for bands blatantly more dangerous than KISS. I also know salesmen who have outsold Mr. Popeil. Gene Simmons and Ron, however, were first to stake their claim and anyone who would dare to challenge their monikers would be doing them a service by helping them build their legends even further. The burden of the proof would rely on the challenger. Don't fall into the trap of making a claim so small your competitors would have no need to knock you down, as you've already done it yourself. If your competition is gunning for you, it's because they perceive you on a higher rung of the ladder and see you as a threat to their survival. What more could an MSV ask for?

PART III

THE MOMENT
OF TRUTH:

33: RESCUE IS NOT COMING

"This job would be great if it weren't for the F'N customers."
—Randal Graves, Clerks

The above quote used to live rent-free in my brain. I would constantly be thinking, "If I could only get a few clients who had it all together, life would be grand."

The easy mindset is to continue doing the great work you've always done. Surely someone will discover it and usher you into the aspirational world of amazing, fulfilling work for clients who have their shit together.

Sadly, these clients rarely exist.

If you think you are the exception, let's take a look at Rick Rubin. Rick is a music producer who popularized hip hop. Not limited to just that single genre, he has also produced, resurrected careers, discovered, or catapulted acts to superstardom such as Beastie Boys, Johnny Cash, Slayer, Red Hot Chili Peppers, and countless more. *Time* named him one of the most influential people in the world, and MTV called him the most important producer in the past 20 years.

Rick is considered not only the gold standard in music production but also a guru. He is a mild-mannered, shaman-like character with a long white beard, roaming about his Malibu property and studio, drinking up all that is beautiful and creative. Surely a man of such accomplishment, acclaim and adoration should be free and clear of the whims of crazy, temperamental clients, right? Enter Kanye West.

In part three of the Netflix documentary *Jeen-Yuhs*, you can witness the birth of one of the greatest MSVs the world has ever known. Sadly, it's only via speakerphone, so we can't see Rick physically rolling his eyes, but goddamn we can sure hear it. Those of us who are attuned to the worlds of creativity and supervillainy can read Rick's innermost thoughts as the primal scream of "THIS F'N INDUSTRY OF MINE!!!"

Kanye corrects Rick's usage of the word "excited" after he uses it to express his feelings about meeting up with Mr. West. He continues his rant on how the media misuses the word when describing agitated situations in the community, citing additional inane examples. He encourages Rick to use the word "energized" instead.

Rick, ever the consummate professional, placates Kanye and agrees. "I love it," he says. "Always love learning new things." Rough translation: "Go fuck yourself, Kanye."

I mention this somewhat cynical tale to explain that there is no brass-ring client to strive for. If one of the most influential creative people on the planet is not immune to crazy clients, what hope is there for the rest of us? We might as well handle them with the proper mindset—the mindset of an MSV.

The ignorant ones hope to be saved from the crazies in their industry. They live as one of Snidely Whiplash's victims, tied to the railroad tracks, hoping to be saved by the hero. You are far from a victim. You know that there is no hero to save you from the crazies. They exist and always will. It's up to your MSV powers to manage them in a way that doesn't disrupt your day.

Wondering how? Let's get into it in the next chapter.

34: EARNED ARROGANCE

*"The type of clients you have now are indicative of
how you are currently doing business."*
—Unknown

I cannot think of a single villainous colleague who oozes
desperation. Whether you are approaching a plot to overthrow
a government to secure prime real estate for your supervillain's
lair (inside the mouth of their local volcano) or pitching a new
marketing idea in a boardroom, they are *not* thinking, "God, I hope
they go for my plan!"

As a lifelong MSV student, I'm certain you have read books on
pitching and negotiating and collected some key phrases to give you
the higher ground. In fact, you should know more about your field
of marketing than the companies that hire you. Arrogance is a trait
synonymous with supervillains but rest assured: while a healthy
dose of arrogance is vital, it also *must* be earned.

Let's go deeper into the proper mindset of how earned
arrogance can drastically improve your standing in the world (and
how it differs from "asshole arrogance").

Join me, for a moment, in this thought experiment. By some bizarre twist of fate, in an attempt to gain new superpowers, you exposed yourself to gamma waves. Something in your calculations went wrong and now you have an incurable, terminal disease.

You run to the internet to find answers. You uncover a single person who has the cure for that weird glowing green orb that appeared in the center of your chest cavity. You use his contact form for more information, eventually setting up a videoconference. He explains his procedure to you, and you believe he has your solution. Here's my question. As the call comes to an end, who says, "Thank you for your time"?

Most would answer that *you* would thank him for the value he brought to you.

Now let's flip the scenario. An owner's business is about to go under. In an effort to save his flailing venture, he heads to the internet and uncovers you as the sole person who has differentiated yourself to become the best in the world at what you do. You are the only person who can save his business. You explain your value proposition on a Zoom call. The call comes to an end. Do you revert to thanking him for his time and letting you pitch your services to him? Sure, it may be a simple social habit to thank someone for their time, even though *your time* and *your expertise* have been utilized.

What I'm addressing here is the MSV mindset.

Until you enter a sale with the mindset of an MSV, your initial conversation will set the wrong tone for this relationship. Without an MSV mindset, you will continue to feel like the vendor, seeking approval from your client in the form of a signed contract. You will sacrifice your dignity to get a deposit in the bank.

It's been over 25 years since I was in an actual classroom. I've forgotten most of what I was supposed to remember, but one statement resonates with me to this day. It was from a web development class I attended. The professor brought up a website that, at the time, was revolutionary. As he took us through the features and marveled at the accomplishment of the developer, he uttered: "If you can do this type of work, you could walk into any ad agency and tell them you got out of prison that morning, and they'd still hire you." Just like that, my internal quality barometer was set.

Maybe you didn't go to the best college. Maybe you don't have a well-connected network. Maybe you never launched your own brand before. A surefire shortcut to gaining earned arrogance is properly differentiating yourself.

Creating a unique offering that no one else in the market can match will not only separate you from the masses but it will also kick-start you on the path to the true mindset of the MSV. This mindset is the byproduct of having spent an inordinate amount of time thinking about, molding and shaping your work. You'll inspect it from every angle. This deep level of work results in an ironclad confidence in yourself and your products. This is how you create your own personal supervillain domain to reign over. *This* is earned arrogance: never having to raise your voice about your excellence. Everyone has no choice but to lean forward with their full attention.

At the other end of the spectrum, asshole arrogance is where wannabe, amateur MSVs dwell. Think of the uncreative tackiness of online social media "gurus" who shoot videos in front of expensive cars. Asshole arrogance screams, "I know more than you, I have more than you, so you need to listen to me." That's simply the attitude of an insecure jerk. Instead, *your* earned arrogance resonates from a place of "I've studied and honed my craft to the best of my ability." This earned arrogance *requires, without request,* that your client listen to you.

The world does not need any more marketers. It needs highly skilled MSVs. Become one who is so compelling that even if a potential client does pass on your services, they can't help but think, "I wonder what would have happened if I hired that guy?"

MSV Exercise

If you feel as if you are providing true, unequivocal value to your prospects, I invite you to try this exercise. The next time you are rehearsing a presentation for a new prospect, when you get to the slide in your deck with the title WHO WE ARE—you know, the one with all of your headshots, accolades and awards on it—create a slide that simply says:

WHO WE ARE: WHO CARES?

Then continue to explain to your soon-to-be client that by the end of this presentation, your goal is to demonstrate your unique value with so much clarity that it wouldn't matter if that slide contained mugshots of war criminals. The client would still feel compelled to hire you.

I dare you. I double dare you.

Whether you put this slide in your actual presentation depends on how diabolical you truly are. If you do, I can guarantee the absence of glazed-over eyes. At the very least, this rehearsal exercise will put you in the proper mindset. It's a mindset that will not have you thanking others for letting you show the value *you* can provide for *them*.

35: IT'S BEEN INSIDE YOU ALL ALONG

"The only thing standing between you and your goal is the bullshit story you keep telling yourself as to why you can't achieve it."

—Jordan Belfort, The Wolf of Wall Street

Spidey Sense is the extraordinary ability to sense imminent danger made popular by comic book superhero Spider-Man. Now before you go out and try to level the playing field by getting bitten by radioactive insects or exposing yourself to gamma rays, let it be known you already have this ability deep inside of you.

Dear Marketing Supervillain, it's been inside you all along!

We've all experienced the following scenario. You design a beautiful, professional brand/logo for a client. They show it to everyone they know and receive "valuable" feedback from the masses, including from their dentist (true story!). The revisions come back. They absolutely destroy your finely tuned color palette and layout, which you so eloquently crafted in accordance with the golden ratio. You want to tell the client that both the communal feedback, as well as those critiques generated in the annals of their own mind, just plain suck and will result in fewer sales. But my friend, design is subjective . . . or is it?

Are you too invested in your own hard work to accept outside perspectives? Or are you factually correct? Answer: MSVs are always correct! Those hairs standing up on the back of your neck every time a client utters the words "make my logo bigger" is your version of Spidey Sense.

This finely tuned raw nerve inside your subconscious is real. The rage it is signaling needs to come to the surface but not in a whiny designer rant. So, let's back it up with science (while simultaneously sounding like a complete badass authority).

A study was done where groups of participants were asked to follow a set of simple directions. Each group received the same instruction cards but with increasingly worse and worse font choices, the type of fonts no self-respecting designer would ever choose in a tasteful design. With each participating group, even though the instructions were easy to follow, the groups with the poorest choice of fonts were proven to follow the directions the worst, even growing a sense of apathy for their simple task and leaving out steps altogether where earlier groups pridefully followed the instructions to a tee.

Recently, academic science has begun to accept the power of the unconscious on our decision-making. This unspoken need for clear, professional design is known as the Fluency Effect. It states that if the form of information is difficult to assimilate, it affects our judgment of the substance of the information. *[Peter Sheridan Dodds et al., "An Experimental Study of Search in Global Networks," Science 301 (August 8, 2003): 827-29]*

For example, if a box of frozen pizza has horrible branding and photos, our brains assume it must taste bad. This proven, psychological theory can make a major difference in your overall branding and marketing campaigns.

Unless you are working in a vacuum, design and marketing concepts need to be (and should be) shared, presented and discussed before launching them onto the world. The sheer thought of this presentation process can bring any proud MSV to their knees with anxiety. Since the nature of design is purely subjective, people (the client) will happily throw their knee-jerk reactions and ideas into the mix as they think there are no wrong answers.

Hearing client revisions may leave you doubting your abilities, questioning the sanity of the stakeholders, or being unable to articulate your feelings about their revisions. Such an interaction can result in you storming out of the meeting in a rage. While your emotions may run wild, know that in this situation, you are likely not the emotional basket case you think you are. Because you function at a much higher level than your non-designer counterparts, your emotional reaction is bolstered by science and logic. Keen MSVs have described achieving proper fluency as "scratching an OCD itch that sends tingles through their bodies."

The superpower I call Designer/Marketer Spidey Sense is already inside you. Now you just need to trust and nurture it. Armed with this knowledge, you can now better avoid the menial spats about who really has better taste, you or the client. The next time they inevitably ask you to make their logo bigger, simply clear your throat, remove your glasses, and as you clean the lenses with your shirt flap, look at them with your most academic expression and say, "Sorry, that choice doesn't coincide with the psychological theories of the Fluency Effect."

MSV exit stage left.

36: YOU'RE WAY AHEAD OF YOUR TIME

"The best way to serve your audience is to ignore them."
—Rick Rubin

I magine this. While our friend Temen from Chapter 9 is inventing marketing and branding with his 16th-century Mesopotamian cohorts, you are out walking the Ethiopian mountainside with your goats. You notice your herd get an inordinate amount of energy after they eat some weird berries from what has become their new favorite bush.

After some days of trial and error, you create a new drink that helps people stay awake longer, get more things done, and essentially gives them "more life." To top it all off, your creation doesn't taste half bad. You proudly introduce your elixir to the world. The reaction? Society immediately shuns you and your drink.

The few who do openly enjoy it are also vilified because your drink elicits a new state of mind, an unnamed form of drunkenness. Soon, your beverage is outright banned by powerful conservative religious sects, such as the Ethiopian Orthodox Church.

The goat herder in question was named Kaldi, and as you may have guessed, his creation was coffee. Kaldi was clearly a renegade of his time and, like most forward-thinkers, he was chastised and made an outcast. Yet, while his legacy is centuries old, he is a prime example of the ultimate MSV.

It would be great to simply shrug off the masses by blaming their reactions on their primitive, puny minds. It simply does not seem that the human mind has had much evolution when facing something new, improved, or truly differentiated. Humankind as a whole often claims it is tired of the status quo and that it would gleefully celebrate those who think outside the box. Sadly, as MSVs, we know this is not at all true.

This is brutally clear in the public's television viewing preferences. They pine for something out of the ordinary but quickly retreat to the tired, tried and "true" formats on other television sitcoms.

All in the Family, The Mary Tyler Moore Show, Friends and *Seinfeld* are all shows that delivered on what television executives asked for because of what viewing audiences demanded. They broke the format of what was typically expected to be broadcast and provided viewers with something truly different.

The result?

Focus groups, created by the network, rated *All in the Family* extremely poorly. *The Mary Tyler Moore Show* shocked the creators when it actually scored even worse than *All in the Family*. *Friends* and *Seinfeld*? Test audiences hated them outright. Luckily, thanks to some rare forward-thinking executives, these shows were given enough life support to mature into the upper echelon of the most successful sitcoms ever created.

So here we sit, forward-thinking marketers and differentiators whose ideas are ahead of our time, some of which even terrify the general public. Like Kaldi, we may have our creations shunned—or, if we are supremely lucky, outright banned.

The fact is that our amazing outside-the-box campaigns may be shelved by the exact boardroom who languished for something "new, fresh, and truly different."

To quote Lloyd Kaufman, our Troma hero from Chapter 25:

"Life isn't safe, if you're born different, tough shit, the world hates different because it's scary and unsafe. They need safety, they want McDonald's, and they want Tom Cruise movies. To live as a differentiator, you have to live according to what you believe. You may fail, get killed or even chop off your own ear, but one thing I can guarantee is it won't be safe." (*All I Need to Know About FILMMAKING I Learned From THE TOXIC AVENGER: The Shocking True Story of Troma Studios*)

37: STANDING OUT WHEN YOU CAN BARELY STAND UP

"There's no easy way out. There's no shortcut home."
—Robert Tepper

It's time to get down to business and put in some work. Understandably, you may have a few rounds of concerns about the monumental task at hand. Just like that potentially exhausting workout on your schedule, the business of differentiating yourself in your industry can seem insurmountable.

We've all experienced those times where we just weren't motivated to take on that hard work. You may have a motivational Spotify playlist to help pump you up. For me, I usually watch one of the greatest sports films ever: *Rocky III*. The third installment of the Sylvester Stallone–led franchise tells the story of a champion whose lifestyle of wealth and idleness is suddenly shaken when a powerful fighter challenges him.

Rocky turns to a former adversary, Apollo Creed, to help rebuild him both mentally and physically so he can reclaim what was once his. Allow me to be your own personal Apollo Creed and see if I can utilize my experience to address some of your objections.

ROUND 1: "I don't want to lose what I already have!"

After losing the title to Clubber Lang, Rocky was not only defeated physically but mentally as well. Apollo tries motivating Rocky with logic, then hounds him, and finally taunts him, but nothing works. The duo has a breakdown and Rocky finally has to admit to himself and the world that he is scared.

Early in his career, he had nothing. It was just him in the ring, taking a beating. He was okay with that; nothing else mattered. Now with a wife and kids, Rocky is no longer alone in the fight, and he is afraid of losing what he already has.

This is an extremely valid concern and one you must weigh carefully. Properly differentiating yourself will require sacrifice. It is not my place to weigh these vital and likely frightening concerns for you. I will, however, issue a word of caution. There is a popular mantra about not being afraid to fail. I disagree. Be afraid to fail—it is human to be afraid. Let that fear motivate you, not intimidate you. What is scarier than failing is living a life of question. Deep down, you are a champion of your industry. Champions lose on occasion, but they lose without leaving any stone unturned and no what-ifs on the table.

ROUND 2: "I don't have the time to learn a new skill set. Hell, at this point in my career, I don't think I even want to."

For your entire career, you've been killing it. But now you find yourself as the challenger, the underdog. What got you to where you are is no longer getting the job done. Champions continually hone their skills, but with a long career behind you, you may simply be tired.

Maybe someone else came along and ate your lunch by doing what you do, just better. Or you've become disillusioned with the market because it has set the bar so low no one cares about your stellar value-adds. So you switched gears. You were playing not to lose, but now you must shift and play to win. Running your business defensively is a strategy. Statistically, however, sports teams that play good offense beat great defense-minded teams much more often.

Successful differentiation requires new skills and disciplines to reposition your business so that you are primed for outstanding results. Education and training are an ongoing process. Someone in your industry is harvesting new information. Someone in your industry is growing. Is it you or your competitor? If the ostrich is your brand mascot, you've got a problem. Playing it safe or putting it off until tomorrow is always tempting. But as Apollo tells Rocky, "There is no tomorrow!" Get your MSV ass out there and learn.

ROUND 3: "I don't have a 'this effing industry of mine' story. Maybe I'm part of the problem?"

"Oh my god, I stand for nothing!"

I've heard very smart, accomplished people, with decades of experience in their respective fields, cry this out when asked what their contrasting or unique perspective on their industry was. It clearly represented a breakdown in their plan and motivation. What they realized was that at some time in their career, they got soft and went on autopilot. Now, the rest of the pack has caught up to them.

Apathy is now firmly in the driver's seat. And apathy is the most dangerous driver because it lacks direction and, well, *drive*! Apollo tries motivating Rocky by telling him to find his passion again, to become the hungry predator that he once was. Eye of the tiger! Eye of the tiger, Rocky!

While breakdowns can be petrifying, you possess the strength to face them head-on with discipline and rigor. Breakdowns are also opportunities for incredible breakthroughs, once you can find your own personal Eye of the Tiger.

ROUND 4: "I don't have the guts to be differentiated."

If you identified with this statement, let me forewarn you, this part is going to be difficult to read and accept. It's reality check time and your reality is staring you in the face. It is personified by the genetically and chemically enhanced killing machine, Ivan Drago from *Rocky IV*.

If you are making big enough changes to your brand's positioning, you should feel scared. (And if not, you're not thinking big enough.) But during Rocky's reality check, Adrian says, "You're a fighter, so fight!" You've spent your career preaching to others about standing out in the crowd, about differentiation. Now is the time when the rubber meets the road. For you to thrive in the new landscape of your industry, you need to heed your own advice.

Will it take courage? Absolutely.

Will it feel uncomfortable? Yes, very much in the same way your clients experience your marketing strategies.

Will you need to put up a fight just to survive? One hundred percent. It's going to be the fight of your life.

But take note: Drago is not out to hurt you personally. He's not a man. He's a machine keen on destroying everything you have ever built and any path toward your ultimate success.

What are you going to do? You're a fighter, so fight!

ROUND 5: "Things aren't great, but I'm close enough to retirement. I don't want to shake that hornet's nest."

Fair enough. Close the book now and enjoy Boca Raton and the early bird specials. Your ship has a hole in it, but you, the captain, have decided to abandon all the women and children. You may have missed the point of the book and have taken your supervillain role too seriously. My only request is with a boring, submissive ending to your story, please do not decide to write a book. The world has enough tomes penned by those who have retired without any scars.

THE FINAL ROUND:

Sure, you've been knocked down. But like the Champ says, "It's not about how hard you hit. It's about how hard you can get hit and keep moving forward." And MSVs *always* get back up.

So, turn on your playlist because "I didn't hear no bell." Let's get to work!

38: THE MOMENT OF TRUTH

"The struggle you are facing is a test to see if you are truly committed to the life you say you want."

—Bobby Axelrod, Billions

I've often heard the following statements when I challenge clients to differentiate their brand:

- "We're an anomaly, there's nothing different about us."
- "Our industry has always promoted the same _____ (insert nouns here)."
- "People don't really care if we are different; they just want the lowest price or the fastest service." (Warning! That last one is *exactly* the definition of a commodity and *why* you must differentiate!)

This is the moment of truth. The blade of death is spinning closer and closer to your neck. Perhaps now you're starting to think those insane clients who ask to be taken to the edge, peek over it, and panic back to a position of safety may not be so insane after all. The life of marketing supervillainy isn't for everyone.

Before you retreat back to joining the legions of mundane, middle-of-the-road marketing masses, consider this final thought experiment:

How much would you pay for something you could get for free?

"I'd pay *nothing!*" is the knee-jerk reaction everyone immediately spouts, and thus the exercise begins.

Let's take a look at the ultimate commodity: water.

With the simple twist of a faucet, water in the industrialized world is readily available and free. Yet consumers continue to throw down dollar after dollar for bottle after bottle as corporations enjoy profits over profits—over $20 billion in 2021. But hey, it comes from a spring at the top of a melting glacier in Fiji, Vermont, Mount Kilimanjaro, or whatever magical place you desire. Yet according to Ecowatch's report, 64% of bottled water comes from the same public reservoirs as our tap water.[4] It's just been rebranded by some MSVs to get us to pay for it.

The hard-earned dollar you've exchanged for bottled water may not have been for the liquid at all. In fact, you are paying for many of its byproducts (remember that planet?). You're paying for the convenience of not lugging around a bucket of the free stuff you filled at your kitchen sink that morning, easier portion control, or the refrigeration of the beverage the store provides while you are on the run.

The list goes on, and the exercise helps change the mindset of business owners on their path to uncovering their true industry differentiators.

Let's up the ante on this exercise.

How could I get you to pay over $500 million for a company whose product revenue for the abundant commodity of water was just $49 million? Before you run to your accountant for a tutorial on profit-loss balance sheets and multiples on evaluation, I'll give you a hint: you must decommoditize that commodity through—you guessed it—differentiation.

Throughout the entire process of writing this book, I've been looking the most forward to talking about one of my favorite modern differentiated brands: Liquid Death, a new (at the time of writing) canned mountain water brand that sees less than 10% of its valuation in annual sales.

Liquid Death is a poster child for differentiation, ticking off multiple boxes on our Universe of Differentiation worksheet (and doing it very well, I might add). Owner Mike Cessario gleefully admits that the company is 90% brand—a brand that is essentially a punch line or a joke to the small, segmented audience of millennials who "get it."

Cessario has built an impressive empire by ensuring every marketing decision answers the question "Would Slayer think this is cool?"

If the answer is yes, then Mike executes (pun intended). It is this North Star (or pentagram) that has inspired outlandish social media marketing that comically juxtaposes water as "The Most Dangerous Drink in the World." It has differentiative craft brewery-style packaging in metal, tallboy cans, purposely disrupting an entire industry that designs their packaging to resemble, as Mike would put it, "yoga accessories."

Yes, Liquid Death is a rare Cinderella story, perhaps clad in leather and thigh-high heels. I could go on and on about how, among a mountain of notable accomplishments, their irreverent marketing led them in under two months to surpassing industry giant Red Bull in Facebook followers.

But we're here to talk about *you* developing the ability to differentiate *anything*. It's not a process for normal folk, but hey, you're a Marketing Supervillain.

Aren't you?

39: THE MARKETING SUPERVILLAIN MANIFESTO

"Because he's the hero Gotham deserves,
but not the one it needs right now.
So we'll hunt him. Because he can take it."

—Lt. James Gordon, The Dark Knight

Heroes and villains alike all need a code by which they live. Should you feel yourself wavering in your commitment to the MSV lifestyle or unable to deal with being hunted by those resistant to change, refer to the declaration of policy below, aka the MSV Manifesto.

#1: I HAVE A CONTRASTING PERSPECTIVE ON MY MARKETPLACE.

I've tried the traditional path and, well, it simply wasn't right for me.

I am the catalyst of the REVOLUTION of my industry.

#2: I AM NOT HERE TO DO WHAT HAS ALREADY BEEN DONE.

I do not look to others for inspiration. Others look to me.

#3: I PAY NO ATTENTION TO GUARDRAILS.

Guardrails are there to keep people on the paved road. I have no interest in following the same road as the masses. I pave my own pathway. I lead the way for others by seeing the madness in my industry and reshaping it.

#4: MY TACTICS WILL SURELY ATTRACT CRITICISM FROM THE AVERAGE MASSES.

I accept these critiques. The unknowing always criticize that which they don't know or understand. That is their problem, not mine.

#5: I DO NOT MAKE EXCUSES.

I create new paradigms to get to the top, and I am willing to sacrifice to get there.

#6: I HAVE ZERO INTEREST IN CREATING DRAMA FOR THE SAKE OF DRAMA.

When I create drama, I create it for the sake of creating business.

#7: I WILL NOT CHANGE MY VISION TO MEET THE EXPECTATIONS OF THE WORLD.

I will change the world to match my vision.

EPILOGUE: A CALL TO ARMS

*"Differentiating yourself will no doubt draw
criticism from the average folk . . .
But who cares? You tried being average and it sucked."*

—Me

I told you. We're not so different after all.

Now it's your turn. You've been tied to that table for over a hundred pages. The blade of that hypothetical circular saw is awfully close to your hypothetical nether regions. Of course, I'm not going to let you just die. I'm not wasting my glorious monologue on a corpse. But here are the determinant questions:

Will you simply continue down the beaten path that got you into this peril in the first place? Will you applaud yourself for reading another book about marketing, feeling a kindred spirit with the rants of another tortured soul?

Or will you finally act? Will you throw down the gauntlet and finally realize you must take up the fight against everything wrong with "this effing industry of yours"?

I implore you to choose the latter. Is it the easy path? No; MSVs don't take the easy path. (You did carefully read the MSV Manifesto in the previous chapter, didn't you?)

Just remember, I work alone. You'll have to set out on *your* quest by *yourself.* If you plan on following in my footsteps, you missed the point of the entire book. I'm a differentiator, and as such, there's no one like me. *And* there's no one like you.

My path was a perfect path for one single person: me. By the time you figure out my success, I'll already be onto the next big thing. My path can't be your path. But at the very least, you now know that a path exists. As such, that should fuel you with hope and motivation. You'll need to carve *your own* path through all of the necessary challenges. Some of those obstacles will be in sand. Others will be in granite. Continue forward and birth *your* MSV, one villainous step at a time.

Now we come full circle, from one U.S. president to another, with over a century in between them. I began this book with a tale of George Washington and will close with the words of another president whose likeness is etched into the side of Mount Rushmore, Theodore Roosevelt.

Like any truly great villain, Roosevelt was a visionary with a contrasting perspective on the world. Many people feared his appointment to the vice presidency. As U.S. Senator Mark Hanna put it, there was "only one life between that madman and the Presidency."

Roosevelt was an authentic and steadfast supervillain. Most great villains will eventually have the masses love them for the exact reason they hated them in the first place. The villain doesn't change, nor do their ideas or original vision. The world simply changes around them to match their vision. (See MSV Manifesto point #7.)

Should you have a different vision for your marketing, your brand, or even your entire industry, you have a mission and a responsibility to get your ideas out into the world. It will not be easy. Your ideas may be unpopular. As marketers, it is our job to influence what people buy, which means influencing how they feel and think. It's perfectly normal to give a shit about what people think about your process. You may choose to listen to the siren song of feedback, but don't let it pull you to your untimely demise. Don't let the naysayers diminish your commitment to changing your industry. It takes a strong will, intestinal fortitude, and a solid plan to bring your dreams to fruition and prove the doubters wrong.

In case you have been really paying attention and are wondering, I managed to avoid the dystopian future of "Live, Laugh, Love" like the idiot who coasts through a mundane existence with a bland, vanilla girl at my side who likes everything but stands for nothing. As a matter of fact, my wife has a quote tattooed across her body from *The Big Orange Splot*, the children's book on the joys of being different. She reminded me that I posed questions to you at the beginning of this rant for which I never provided, in her words, "a payoff."

Yes, I avoided a milquetoast livelihood. I built a personal brand based upon my outlier passions and shed the brand of a generalist. The ultimate payoff came just two years ago when I received a call. The voice on the other side expressed their seemingly insurmountable business problems and tagged the conversation with "You're the only guy who could possibly solve this thing." (And I did.)

In closing, I leave you with some words from our supervillainous president Theodore Roosevelt:

It is not the critic who counts; not the man who points out how the strong man stumbles, or where the doer of deeds could have done them better. The credit belongs to the man who is actually in the arena, whose face is marred by dust and sweat and blood; who strives valiantly; who errs, who comes short again and again, because there is no effort without error and shortcoming; but who does actually strive to do the deeds; who knows great enthusiasms, the great devotions; who spends himself in a worthy cause; who at the best knows, in the end, the triumph of high achievement, and who at the worst, if he fails, at least fails while daring greatly, so that his place shall never be with those cold and timid souls who neither know victory nor defeat.

Jesse James Wroblewski

ACKNOWLEDGMENTS:

Nick Ambrosino: For trudging through all of my pop culture references and basically co-writing this thing.

Brendan Bailey: The best damn henchman a guy could ask for.

Florence Ivy: The trophy wife.

You will all be spared and I will reserve a comfy pet bed for all of you once my rise to power is fully realized.

ABOUT THE AUTHOR:

J esse James Wroblewski has been at the helm of a NY marketing
agency for close to three decades. His often offbeat work has
been featured in *Rolling Stone,* the book *505 Weirdest Websites Ever*
and the long-running horror film fan magazine *Fangoria,* as well as a
plethora of other media outlets.

After the realization that the entire marketing industry had
gone insane, he retooled, reimagined, and reemerged as something
different, something more powerful than the marketing world has
ever seen. Eager to share his new vision with the world and spark a
marketing revolution, he created the call to arms you are holding in
your hands now — *Marketing For Supervillains.*

Jesse lives in a supervillain lair on Long Island, which he has
dubbed Chainsaw Estates, with his trophy wife, Florence. (The
opposite sex is always attracted to danger!)

To learn more or to join this marketing movement, visit:
www.decomoditized.com

ENDNOTES:

[1] Luke Sullivan and Edward Boches, *Hey Whipple, Squeeze This: The Classic Guide to Great Advertising*, 6th edition. New York: Wiley, 2022.

[2] ABC News, Excerpt: "The Wisdom of Ginsu," *Good Morning America*, March 31, 2005. https://abcnews.go.com/GMA/story?id=628580

[3] David C. Baker, "'More Better' Is Not a Strategy." https://www.davidcbaker.com/more-better-is-not-a-strategy

[4] Ecowatch. "Report: 64% of Bottled Water Is Tap Water, Costs 2000x More." February 21, 2018. https://www.ecowatch.com/bottled-water-sources-tap-2537510642.html

Printed in Great Britain
by Amazon